brilliant
Microsoft® Windows XP
POCKET BOOK

Geoff Preston

PEARSON
Prentice Hall

Harlow, England • London • New York • Boston • San Francisco • Toronto
Sydney • Tokyo • Singapore • Hong Kong • Seoul • Taipei • New Delhi
Cape Town • Madrid • Mexico City • Amsterdam • Munich • Paris • Milan

Pearson Education Limited
Edinburgh Gate
Harlow CM20 2JE
Tel: +44 (0)1279 623623
Fax: +44 (0)1279 431059
Website: www.pearsoned.co.uk

Originally published as *A simple guide to Windows XP* by Prentice Hall in 2002

© Pearson Education Limited 2002, 2006

The rights of Gilles Fouchard and Geoff Preston to be identified as authors of this work have been asserted by them in accordance with the Copyright, Designs and Patents Act 1988.

ISBN-13: 978-0-13-328888-9
ISBN-10: 0-13-230088-5

British Library Cataloguing-in-Publication Data
A catalogue record for this book is available from the British Library

All rights reserved. No part of this publication may be reproduced, stored in a retrieval system, or transmitted in any form or by any means, electronic, mechanical, photocopying, recording or otherwise, without either the prior written permission of the publisher or a licence permitting restricted copying in the United Kingdom issued by the Copyright Licensing Agency Ltd, 90 Tottenham Court Road, London W1T 4LP. This book may not be lent, resold, hired out or otherwise disposed of by way of trade in any form of binding or cover other than that in which it is published, without the prior consent of the Publishers.

10 9 8 7 6 5 4 3 2 1
10 09 08 07 06

Typeset in 9.5pt Helvetica by 30
Printed and bound in Great Britain by Ashford Colour Press Ltd., Gosport.

The publisher's policy is to use paper manufactured from sustainable forests.

Brilliant Pocket Books

What you need to know – when you need it!

When you're working on your PC and come up against a problem that you're unsure how to solve, or want to accomplish something in an application that you aren't sure how to do, where do you look? If you are fed up with wading through pages of background information in unwieldy manuals and training guides trying to find the piece of information or advice that you need RIGHT NOW, and if you that find that helplines really aren't that helpful, then Brilliant Pocket Books are the answer!

Brilliant Pocket Books have been developed to allow you to find the info that you need easily and without fuss and to guide you through each task using a highly visual step-by-step approach – providing exactly what you need to know, when you need it!

Brilliant Pocket Books are concise, easy-to-access guides to all of the most common important and useful tasks in all of the applications in the Office 2003 suite. Short, concise lessons make it really easy to learn any particular feature, or master any task or problem that you will come across in day-to-day use of the applications.

When you are faced with any task on your PC, whether major or minor, that you are unsure about, your Brilliant Pocket Book will provide you with the answer – almost before you know what the question is!

Contents

Introduction   x

1   The Windows XP philosophy   1

→ A more user-friendly system   1
- The 32-bit architecture   2
- The Windows XP Registry   3

→ A system plugged into the world   3
→ A version that can be used by anyone   4
→ An intuitive graphics interface   4
→ Plug-and-play technology   8

2   Setting up Windows XP   11

→ Installing Windows XP   12
- Register Now   14

→ Help and Support Center   15
- Maintain your hard disks   17
- Connect to the Internet   20

3   Discovering the interface   21

→ Your workbench: the Windows XP Desktop   21
→ My Computer properties   23
→ The Taskbar   25
→ The Start button   27
→ Smart menus   29
- The Programs menu   30
- The Documents menu   30
- The Search menu   31
- The Help menu   35
- The Run menu   35
- The Shut Down menu   36
- The Taskbar and Start menu   37
- Start menu settings   38

4 Working in Windows XP — 41

- → Changing from one task to another — 41
- → The Recycle Bin — 43
- → Starting a program — 45
  - My Computer — 45
  - Handling files and folders — 46
- → Managing objects with Explorer — 47
- → Properties of objects — 49
- → Shortcuts: the fast way to fetch an object — 50
- → Customizing the Start menu — 51
- → Handling diskettes — 52

5 The Control Panel — 55

- → The Control Panel — 55
- → Accessibility options — 56
  - Keyboard set-up — 57
  - Sound and picture settings — 57
- → Monitor display settings — 58
- → Mouse set-up — 60
- → Joystick set-up — 61
- → Modem settings — 62
- → Date and time management — 63
- → Sound management — 63
- → Multimedia set-up — 63
- → Printer management — 65
- → Font management — 66
- → Mail management — 67
- → Connecting to the Internet — 67
- → Creating a password — 68
- → Adding applications — 69
- → The Add Hardware Wizard — 70

6 Windows XP tools — 71

- → The Calculator — 71
- → Notepad — 71
- → Word-processing in WordPad — 72
- → The Paint program — 73
- → The Phone Dialer — 74
- → Character Map — 75

→ Remote Desktop Connection ... 76
→ The HyperTerminal utility ... 76

7 Windows XP and the Internet ... 77

→ The Start button ... 77
  − Calling up favourite Web sites ... 77
  − Finding documents on the Web ... 78
  − Paging ... 80
  − Executing a command ... 80
→ The Taskbar ... 81
  − The Quick Launch bar ... 81
  − Adding new toolbars ... 82
  − Creating a toolbar on the Desktop ... 83
→ Windows Explorer ... 84
  − Surfing the Web ... 86
  − Adding a page to Favorites ... 86
  − Sending a Web page by e-mail ... 87
→ The Windows XP Desktop in Web style ... 88
→ Folder settings ... 89
  − Folder display settings ... 89
  − Display settings for all files ... 91
  − Image file management ... 91
  − The My Computer folder ... 93

8 Internet connection and Home Networking ... 95

→ The Internet connection ... 95
→ Setting up a dial-up connection ... 96
→ Home Networking ... 101

9 The Internet Explorer browser ... 105

  − Search facility ... 105
  − Organizing Favorites ... 105
  − Support for multiple connections ... 105
→ Running the browser ... 105
  − Establishing or terminating your Internet connection ... 108
→ Browsing principles ... 109
  − The navigation buttons ... 109
  − The History file ... 111
  − Displaying links ... 111

– Full-screen surfing	112
– Opening Web pages in a new window	112
– The Explorer Bar	114
→ Web surfing	114
→ Managing your favourite Web sites	115
– Storing Favorites	115
– Scheduled downloading from a Web site	117
→ Internet radio	119

10 Electronic mail 121

→ Handling your messages effectively	122
– Creating document folders	123
– Handling the arrival of new messages	123
– Looking up your messages	125
– Transferring a message	126
– Deleting a message	127
– Sorting messages	127
– Drafting a message	127
– Inserting an attachment	129
→ The Address Book	130
– Handling the Address Book	131
– Adding a new contact	131
– Filling in the Address Book automatically	132
– Setting up an electronic mailshot	132
→ Filtering messages	132
→ Reading your mail from more than one computer	133

11 System tools 135

→ Scheduled tasks	135
→ The system software	137
– System Information	138
→ System Restore	139
– Creating a restore point	139
– Tidying up the hard disk	139
– The FAT 32 converter	140
– Defragmenting the hard disk	141
– Checking the disk	141
→ Transferring settings	143

12 Windows XP and multimedia applications — 145

- → AutoPlay mode for CD-ROMs — 146
- → Multimedia utilities — 146
- → Media Player — 146
  - CD Audio — 147
  - Radio — 148
  - Video — 149
  - Portable device — 149
  - The Sound Recorder — 149
  - Overall volume adjustment — 151
- → Plug-ins and players — 151
- → Audio and video — 152
- → Movie Maker — 153
- → Playing DVDs — 155

Introduction

Welcome to the Brilliant Microsoft® Windows XP Pocket Book – a handy visual quick reference that will give you a basic grounding in the common features and tasks that you will need to master to use Microsoft® Windows XP in any day-to-day situation. Keep it on your desk, in your briefcase or bag – or even in your pocket! – and you will always have the answer to hand for any problem or task that you come across.

Find out what you need to know – when you need it!

You don't have to read this book in any particular order. It is designed so that you can jump in, get the information you need and jump out – just look up the task in the contents list, turn to the right page, read the introduction, follow the step-by-step instructions – and you're done!

How this book works

Each section in this book includes foolproof step-by-step instructions for performing specific tasks, using screenshots to illustrate each step. Additional information is included to help increase your understanding and develop your skills – these are identified by the following icons:

Information – This provides you with additional advice on a task or function to improve your understanding and ability to master it.

Timesaver tip – These tips give you ideas that cut corners and confusion. They also give you additional information related to the topic that you are currently learning. Use them to expand your knowledge of a particular feature or concept.

Important – This identifies areas where new users often run into trouble, and offers practical hints and solutions to these problems.

Brilliant Pocket Books are a handy, accessible resource that you will find yourself turning to time and time again when you are faced with a problem or an unfamiliar task and need an answer at your fingertips – or in your pocket!

1 The Windows XP philosophy

Since Windows 95, Microsoft has been simplifying the use of the PC on a day-to-day basis to win over new users and promote the system to all consumers. The major concepts developed for Windows 95 were reproduced in Windows 98 and have been taken a step further with Windows XP. We will go into these in more detail later on.

→ A more user-friendly system

It is no longer necessary for new computer users to learn about DOS (the *disk operating system*): personal computing has moved on. However, applications operating in DOS can still be run, so you will be able to make the most of your old programs and especially all your favourite games.

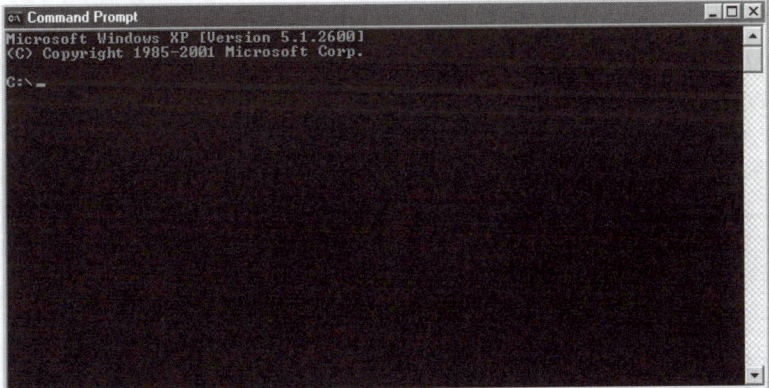

Figure 1.1 The MS-DOS Prompt window.

Information

The DOS prompt If you need to run a program in DOS, find the Command Prompt on the Start menu (it should be in Accessories).

Compatibility with existing systems also includes recognition of the peripheral drivers and the network software. It was important that the system was able to accept the installation of a new item of equipment or peripheral (such as a printer or modem) quickly and easily. This new feature was based on a product strategy known as *Plug-and-Play*, implemented jointly by Microsoft and the leading players in the computer industry.

Although Windows XP is compatible with the existing system with regard to certain matters, this is not the case in terms of performance. The idea of running Windows XP on a 486 PC or even an entry-level Pentium processor is out of the question. In addition, memory (RAM) of 32 Mb is essential in order to run the system. For many existing users, the transition from Windows 3.1 to Windows XP will call for a change of PC.

The 32-bit architecture

The major technical advances, beginning with Windows 95, have been 32-bit architecture and better system resource management, which have created a more powerful, stable system. Windows XP reproduces the 32-bit print manager and graphics manager technology that came with Windows 95 and the 32-bit model (the 32-bit Windows Driver Model – WDM 32) for peripheral drivers and the new file system in 32-bit mode which was introduced with Windows 98.

Windows 3.1 users will also appreciate the multitasking mode of Windows XP, also a feature of Windows 95 and 98/Me, which enables several applications to be run simultaneously.

Important

The 32-bit file system When installing Windows XP (see Chapter 2) on a Windows 95 PC, you can request that your existing Windows and DOS files be retained in order to reinstall them at a later date. You can uninstall Windows XP, provided you have kept the default file management mode. Windows XP is supplied with a system utility (FAT 32 converter), which allows you to change the file manager to 32-bit mode. If you make use of this facility you will not then be able to change back to Windows 95.

The Windows XP Registry

All technical information is stored centrally in a database known as the Registry. This database continually updates the PC configuration, thereby ensuring that Windows XP operates at its best. It also has a role in the Plug-and-Play technology by establishing, each time an item of equipment is installed, which resources are unassigned (IRQ, 1/0 addresses, DMA channels, etc.) and allocating them elsewhere. Another advantage of the Registry is that it bypasses the notorious DOS configuration files AUTOEXEC.BAT and CONFIG.SYS, as well as the Windows 3.1 .INI files. Windows 95 and 98 users have already benefited from this new feature. The Registry can be looked up and modified from a remote location via a network, which is important for business users and DP managers.

→ A system plugged into the world

Under Windows 95, access to remote information servers was greatly enhanced. Access is gained in point-to-point mode or with specialized connection systems. As well as these connections, Windows 95 incorporated a centralized information send-and-receive system called Microsoft Exchange. This system, which supports the MAPI standard, provided a single location from which to retrieve fax messages or e-mail. Although Microsoft Exchange still exists in Windows XP, it is somewhat redundant since e-mail traffic can now be handled by the Internet message system, Outlook Express.

The facility designed for Windows 95 no longer meets the needs generated by the phenomenal development of Internet communications. Windows 95 anticipated this development by adapting its basic architecture: it already incorporated a 32-bit version of the TCP/IP protocol (the communication and interchange protocol used on the World Wide Web). But making a successful Internet connection was a feat in itself. Since then, all possible resources have been deployed to integrate the connection process more effectively; the Internet Connection Wizard, supplied with the Internet Explorer 6.0 software package, now performs that function.

→ A version that can be used by anyone

For novices, Windows XP brings its own clutch of new features and clears up a number of problems encountered in earlier versions of Windows. These significant changes bring the PC within range of a vast number of people, and encourage its adoption by the home user. Here we should note that use of the PC differs greatly between business and domestic environments. Home users can now enjoy the benefits of the new generation of multimedia games, which rely increasingly on sophisticated synthesized animations. To this end, the graphics display standards (*Accelerated Graphics Port* – AGP) are recognized by Windows XP. There is also the opportunity to enjoy easy, rapid Internet access and to use the Internet Explorer 6.0 navigation software to surf the Web, or to join in the discussion forums (*newsgroups*), not to mention the Outlook Express message system to send and receive e-mail. Naturally, the PC running Windows XP, together with its electronic office software, remains an outstanding work tool. With the growth of part-time employment, teleworking and distance learning, the domestic PC bridges the traditional business–home gap.

Windows XP incorporates all the key features that meet the requirements of the general public. It continues to use the features that made Windows 95 and 98 such a success and now incorporates the extra Internet dimension. With Windows XP, computing becomes a genuine pleasure. Here are a few aspects of the system to illustrate this point.

→ An intuitive graphics interface

The Windows XP graphics interface is basically the same as that in Windows 95 and 98, and Me; it may take some time to get used to if you have previously remained faithful to Windows 3.1. The Windows XP interface offers a number of working methods – including the Web (see Chapter 7) – and enables you to customize your own environment. There is more than one way to execute most commands in Windows XP; for example, there are four ways of starting an application or opening a document:

- **Method 1.** Click on the **Start** button, then choose your program or document by selecting **All Programs** (Figure 1.2).

- **Method 2.** Find the program icon on the Desktop, click the right mouse button, and select **Open** from the pop-up menu (Figure 1.3).

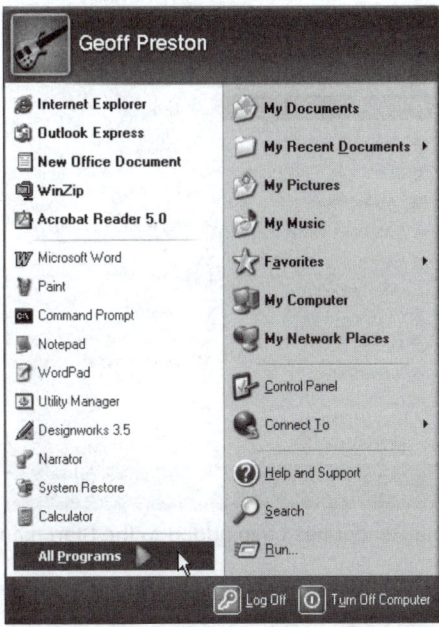

Figure 1.2 Clicking on the **Start** button brings up a list of programs, documents and submenus.

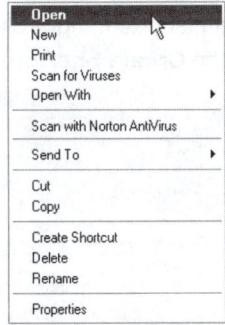

Figure 1.3 Opening a program from the Desktop.

- **Method 3.** Drag the program icon to the Start button; the application will then be entered on the main list under that button and you simply click on it to execute the program (Figure 1.4).

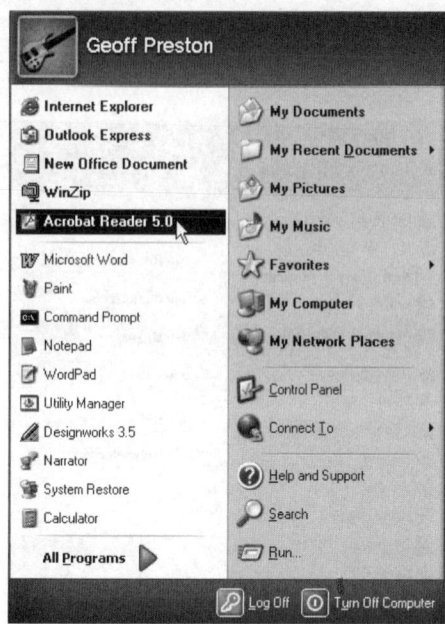

Figure 1.4 Acrobat Reader has been added to the Start menu by a drag-and-drop action.

- **Method 4.** Create a shortcut that can be accessed on the Windows XP Desktop. A shortcut is a quick link to an object (i.e. a program or a document) stored in the PC or accessible via the Internet. A shortcut is recognized by the little folding arrow that appears on the icon. To create a program shortcut, right-click on the program icon in question and select the **Create Shortcut** option (Figure 1.5).

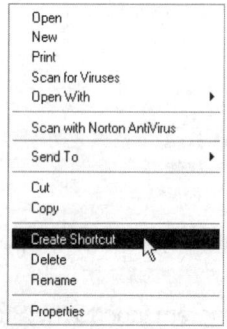

Figure 1.5 The Create Shortcut command.

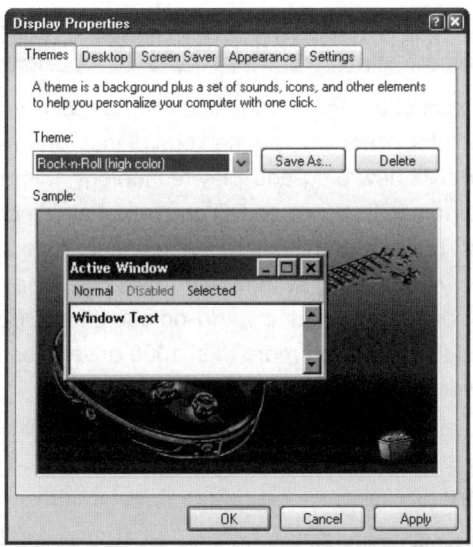

Figure 1.6 Changing the Desktop Theme in Windows XP.

You can change the Windows XP environment to suit your own needs. This is ideal for use in a family context, since the PC can be adapted to children's tastes. You can add background images, change the shape of icons, or even use sound to give a games arcade effect. Windows XP provides a set of desktop user profiles, Microsoft Plus, which previously formed part of the Windows 95 add-on package. To choose a profile, click on **Start**, **Settings**, **Control Panel**. Then select **Desktop Themes**. Now choose the theme and click **OK** (Figure 1.6).

Information

The Windows XP Desktop The Desktop provides the main work screen. On starting up Windows XP, it includes the following items: the Start button, the Taskbar, a number of icons on the Desktop, and an access area to Web channels. The Taskbar is at the bottom of the screen to the right of the Start button. The Desktop icons represent objects or shortcuts to objects. We will discuss these in greater detail later.

→ Plug-and-play technology

While the success of the PC is due mainly to its open-ended flexibility, this is a setback for users who are nervous of installing new equipment. With its new plug-and-play technology, Microsoft has imposed certain specifications on PC and peripherals equipment manufacturers. The aim of this has been to ensure total compatibility with the Windows operating system and to simplify, or even automate, the installation of memory and any add-on equipment. For this reason, Windows XP is supplied with more than 1000 drivers responsible for recognizing over 1000 different devices.

Information

Why plug-and-play? The purpose of plug-and-play is to avoid conflicts such as interrupt handling (IRQ) or memory access management (DMA) by making the installation of equipment much simpler for the user. Plug-and-play technology is based on three PC components: the BIOS on the motherboard, the controllers (ISA, EISA, PCI, PCMCIA, SCSI, etc.) and the operating system itself. The BIOS is a manufacturer's program that determines the hardware configuration of the PC. Each manufacturer must therefore make their BIOS compatible with Microsoft specifications. A plug-and-play BIOS sends Windows XP all the information that might assist the end user.

The Control Panel (**Start**, **Control Panel**, **Printers and Other Hardware**) window contains an Add Hardware link, which guides you through installing new internal (e.g. a graphics board) or external equipment (e.g. a printer or modem) (Figure 1.7).

The Add Hardware Wizard (Figure 1.8) automatically recognizes the new plug-and-play peripherals. If it fails to do so, select a hardware family and use a diskette to install the necessary driver. You can also download the driver from the manufacturer's Internet site.

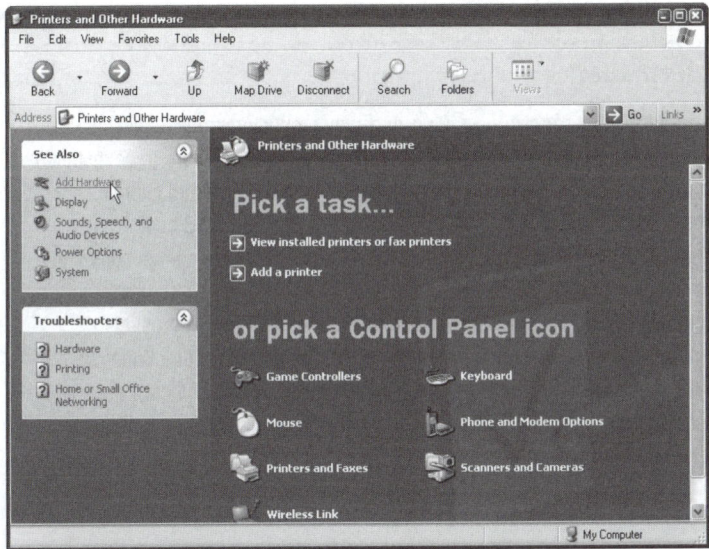

Figure 1.7 Using the Control Panel to add new hardware.

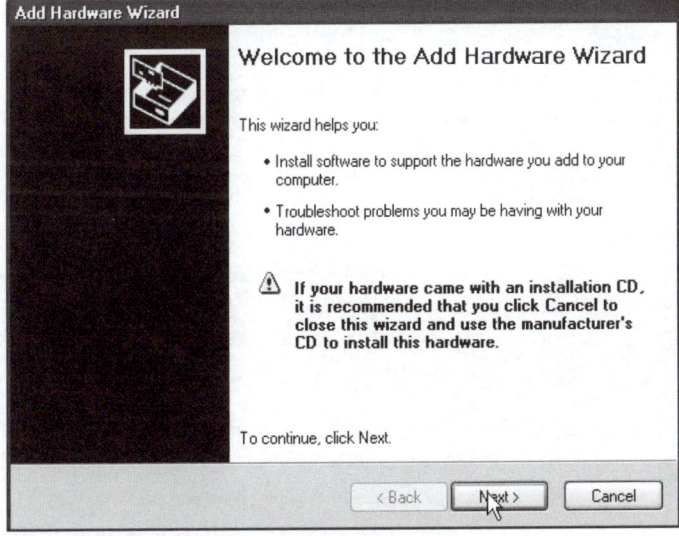

Figure 1.8 Using a wizard to install new hardware.

Information

Plug-and-play technology Plug-and-play technology must satisfy a wide range of constraints. It is of vital importance that the hardware to be installed on a PC can be connected to the majority of known buses and connector types. These include ISA, EISA, VESA Local Bus, PCI and USB buses, and PCMCIA, SCSI and IDE connections, as well as the monitor connections and the serial or parallel ports. This technology must guarantee automatic installation, loading into RAM and the unloading of drivers. It must also enable dynamic (hot) configuration changes that do not require Windows XP to be shut down; this feature allows, for example, a PCMCIA board to be inserted without shutting down the machine. Finally, individual applications must be able to respond to these dynamic configuration changes.

2 Setting up Windows XP

This section is for the benefit of those readers who are upgrading from earlier versions of Windows. If your PC came with Windows XP, move straight on to Help and Support Center (page 15).

Windows XP can be installed directly on a PC running Windows 95 or 98.

> **Important**
>
> **32 Mb for Windows XP** First of all, check that you have at least 32 Mb of RAM – this is a prerequisite for installing Windows XP.

Insert your Windows XP CD-ROM. In Windows 95 or 98, Autorun mode automatically starts up the Windows XP CD-ROM, without the user needing to know the name of the start-up file.

The dialog shown in Figure 2.1 asks whether you wish to upgrade your computer to Windows XP. Click on **Install Windows XP** to start the set-up procedure.

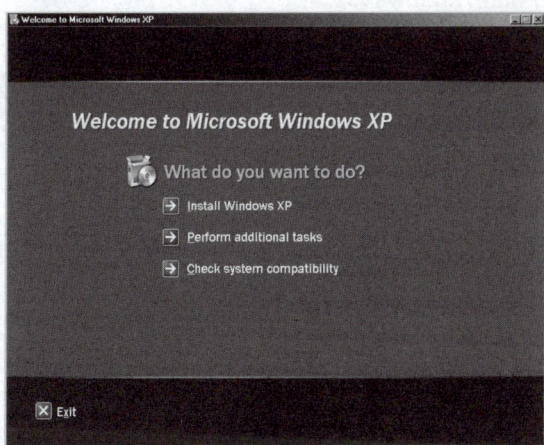

Figure 2.1 The Windows XP welcome screen.

The set-up procedure will now check your system and then prepare the Windows XP Setup Wizard to guide you through the rest of the process.

You may be given a warning that you should close down all Windows programs before continuing. When you have done this, click **Next** to continue the set-up (Figure 2.2).

Figure 2.2 Ready to begin the Setup.

You may first select the compatibility option, which will search through your computer and check that the currently installed programs are compatible with Windows XP.

→ Installing Windows XP

The installation phases are as follows:

- preparing for installation
- collecting information
- copying files on the computer
- rebooting the PC
- hardware installation and final parameter set-up.

The procedure tells you what the average installation time will be (about 45 minutes in most cases). This time is updated at each stage.

> **Information**
>
> **Uninstalling Windows XP** At the start of the installation phase, you can ask to save existing Windows and DOS files in order to re-install them later. You can then uninstall Windows XP. To do this you will need 120 Mb of hard disk space. Click **Yes** at the prompt.

The Windows XP Installation Wizard starts by checking the Registry database and preparing the Windows directory from the beginning.

Installation involves the following steps:

- **Acceptance of the licence agreement**. Click on **Next** to accept the terms.
- **Save system files**. Click on **Yes** to allow you to uninstall Windows XP and revert to your original environment.
- **Creating a start-up diskette**. This enables you to restart your PC if a problem occurs or to run certain diagnostic routines.

As you might expect, Windows XP facilitates Web connections and recognizes the various types of network you can use, especially the high bit rate links such as ISDN. It includes numerous features, which will be described in detail throughout this book; it contains more multimedia and more games than Windows 95 or 98, and is also more user-friendly.

On completion of file copying, the Installation Wizard will reboot your computer.

Preparing for the initial execution of Windows XP may take a further 10 minutes or so. This stage includes building the peripheral database and the detection of plug-and-play components. The latter are installed and recognized correctly by the new system. Over 1000 devices (modems, graphics boards, printer, etc.) are recognized by Windows XP.

The next stage involves installing the elements required for:

- the Control Panel
- Start menu programs
- the Windows Help facility
- DOS program settings

- setting the application start-up routine
- system configuration.

The system then reboots automatically, assembling the driver files required for machine operation.

On completion of the installation process, you will be offered the opportunity to register with Microsoft.

- Register Now
- Connect to the Internet
- Discover Windows XP
- Maintain Your Computer.

Register Now

Click on **Register Now** to access the online Registration Wizard (Figure 2.3). After registering you will be notified of new products and updates, and you will be able to obtain the best possible technical support. You will also be able to access the Windows Update program, the Web extension of Windows XP. This program will keep you up to date by:

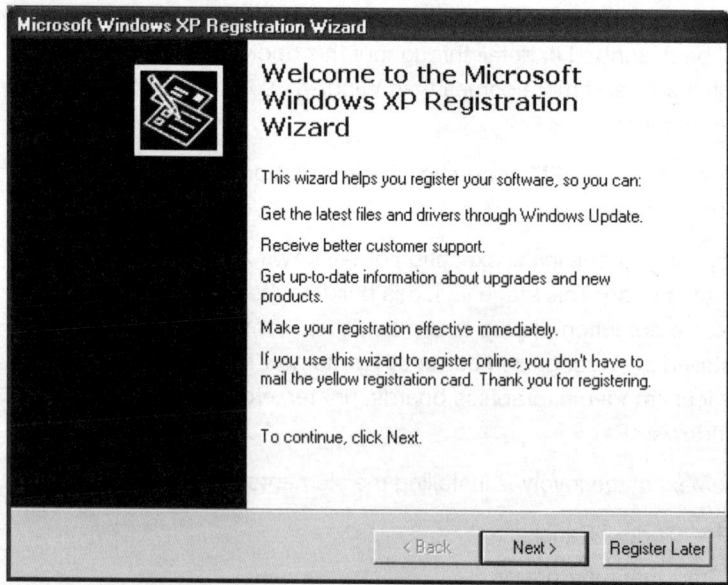

Figure 2.3 The online Registration Wizard.

14 Brilliant Microsoft® Windows XP Pocket Book

- keeping your system updated, by downloading the latest drivers and system files;
- finding quick answers to technical questions you might like to ask.

The Registration Wizard will detect your modem and the communications port to which it is connected, unless you provide this information yourself.

The online Registration Wizard then lists details of your configuration. You can send this list with your registration particulars. Click **Yes** and then click **Next**. Record the identification number of your product, because you will be asked for this whenever you contact Microsoft.

→ Help and Support Center

Windows XP has a comprehensive Help system that covers all the features of the system and provides help at a range of levels, from beginners to experts. In fact, you can use the Help system to turn yourself from a beginner into an expert!

Important

Web-style Help The Windows XP Help system is different from the Help systems that you will meet in applications. This is based on Web pages, which makes it as easy to use as a browser, but it is significantly slower than other systems. Be patient, the Help is worth the wait.

When first started, the Help and Support Center opens at its Home section (Figure 2.4). This works like a contents list. Here, as everywhere in this system, any underlined item acts as a link to another part of the system. Browse through it to see what is available. Click one of the links on the left to get a list of links under that heading. Some of these links will lead on to other lists of links, others will lead directly to a Help page, which will be displayed on the right.

If you know what you want help on, you can find it faster in the Index section. Type in a keyword to find, and you will see the Index entries. Click on one and you will either be shown the related page or be given a small list of pages to choose from.

Setting up Windows XP **15**

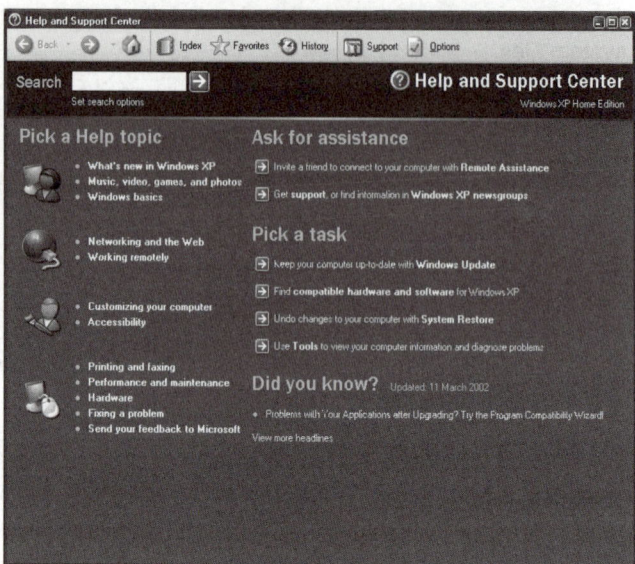

Figure 2.4 Windows XP Help and Support Center open at the Home page.

Before you go much further with Windows XP, you should visit the Tour area (Figure 2.5). Take one of the Tours that introduce Windows XP and its key features.

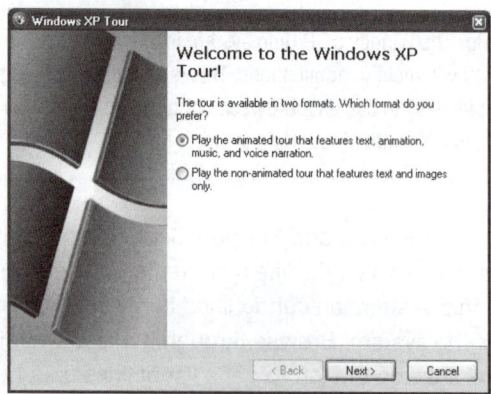

Figure 2.5 Use the Tour to learn more about Windows XP.

Timesaver tip

Search for Help An alternative way to get Help on a topic is to type a keyword into the Search slot and click **Go**.

Brilliant Microsoft® Windows XP Pocket Book

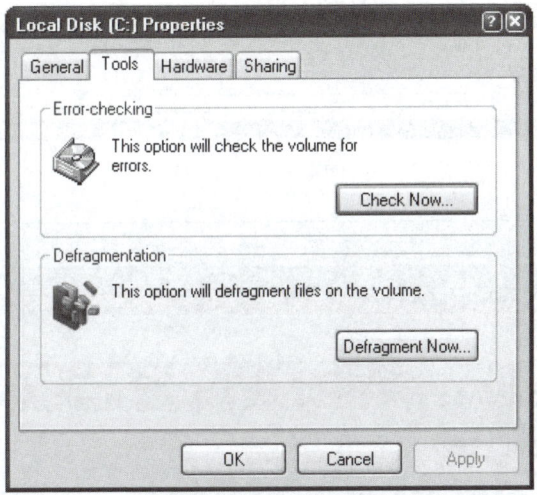

Figure 2.6 Tool dialog offering Error-checking and Defragmentation options.

Maintain your hard disks

There are some tasks that occasionally need to be performed on the hard disk(s). The three disk maintenance procedures are:

- Defragment
- Error checking
- Cleanup.

Open **My Computer** and right-click on the hard disk you wish to work on.

Choose the Defragment option, which leads to a dialog (Figure 2.7).

Information

Defragmenting a hard disk This consists of retrieving vacant spaces and reorganizing data files on your hard disk so that the data in a particular file are contiguous rather than scattered around. The various additions, deletions and modifications you make in the course of your work cause the data in a file to be stored in areas that are not necessarily physically adjacent. As a result, reading a fragmented file becomes a much longer task. Defragmentation involves reorganizing the disk space more rationally, thereby speeding up access.

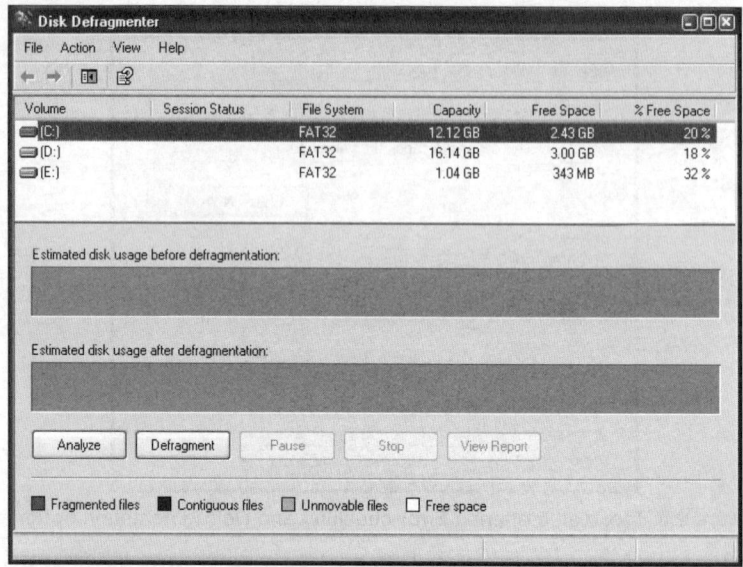

Figure 2.7 Starting defragmentation on drive C.

Defragment

Choose the disk you wish to defragment from the list provided. Clicking the **Analyze** button will provide you with an estimate of its likely benefit. Click the **Defragment** button to begin.

Error checking

This process detects and corrects any errors on your disk drive. Select it from the Properties menu (Figure 2.6) and a window will open (Figure 2.8) offering you the choice of fixing file system errors and/or finding and attempting to repair faults on the surface of the disk.

Disk cleanup

This process removes unwanted files and can generate a huge amount of space. Files which could be removed include:

- temporary Internet files
- downloaded files
- old ScanDisk files stored in the root directory
- temporary files
- temporary installation files
- the contents of the Recycle Bin
- Windows XP uninstall information.

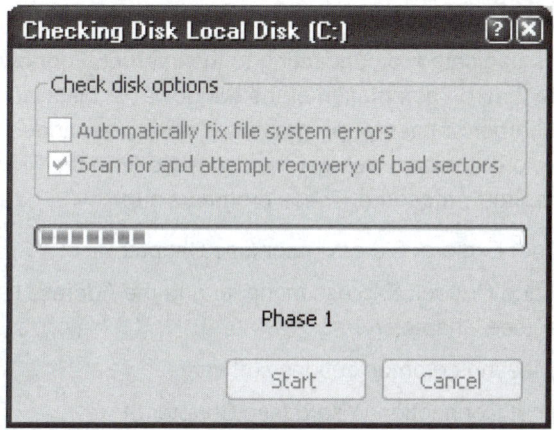

Figure 2.8 Checking drive C for file system errors.

Load Disk Cleanup by clicking on **Start**, opening **All Programs**, choosing **Accessories**, then **System Tools** and then **Disk Cleanup**. The software will calculate how much space can be saved and then you can choose which files you wish to remove (Figure 2.9).

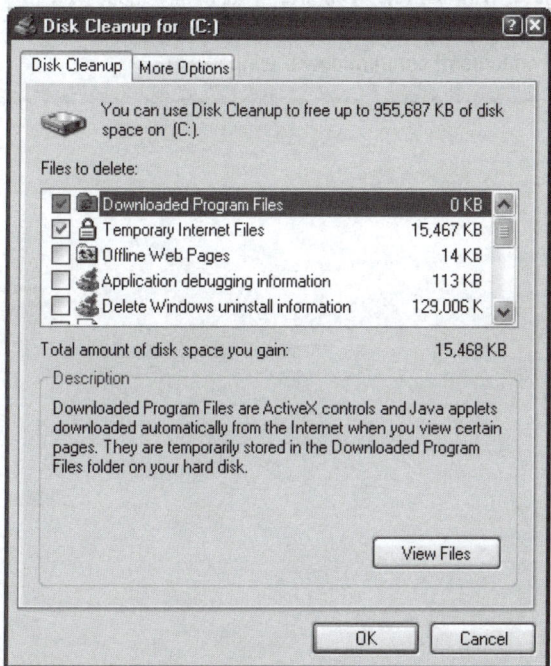

Figure 2.9 Removing unwanted files.

Setting up Windows XP   **19**

Connect to the Internet

Chapter 8 is dedicated to connecting to the Internet. For now you should note that, on completion of the Windows XP installation routine, a number of Internet programs will have been added to the Internet Explorer folder, which can be accessed from the Programs menu in the Start procedure. These programs are:

- the Internet Explorer 6.0 navigator (see Chapter 9)
- the mail and Outlook Express manager and the Address Book manager (see Chapter 7)
- the NetMeeting communications software
- the Internet Connection Wizard (see Chapter 8)
- the Web page creation software, Frontpage Express
- the Web page publication tool, Personal Web Server.

Information

The Microsoft Windows XP Web site To learn more about Windows XP, you can find the Microsoft Web site at the following address:
http://www.microsoft.com/windows/ windowsxp

3 Discovering the interface

With Windows XP, Microsoft wanted not only to meet the needs of new PC users, but also to offer solutions to problems encountered by more experienced users. The Program Manager, File Manager and Print Manager in Windows 3.1 were poorly designed; they have now been replaced by more consistent concepts and tools. Similarly, the Control Panel has been revised and improved. New concepts and a new working philosophy were good reasons for introducing a radically different presentation and operational procedure. Join our guided tour of the Windows XP interface.

→ Your workbench: the Windows XP Desktop

Once you have completed the PC start-up procedure in Windows XP, the workbench, or Desktop, is displayed. The system starts with the default presentation (or display) mode, which you can change later (see Chapter 7) to Web mode. Various icons, distributed about the Desktop, give access to:

- programs (the Internet Explorer navigator, and the Outlook Express message system)
- folders (the online services offered on completion of the installation sequence)
- shortcuts to documents
- resources (My Computer)
- dedicated tools, such as Recycle Bin.

This highly organized Desktop facility conceals all the Windows XP features and the application programs that might have been installed beforehand by the PC manufacturer, and all documents. Do not worry if you have just installed Windows XP on top of Windows 98 or Me: all your tools, programs, texts, images and multimedia files will still be there.

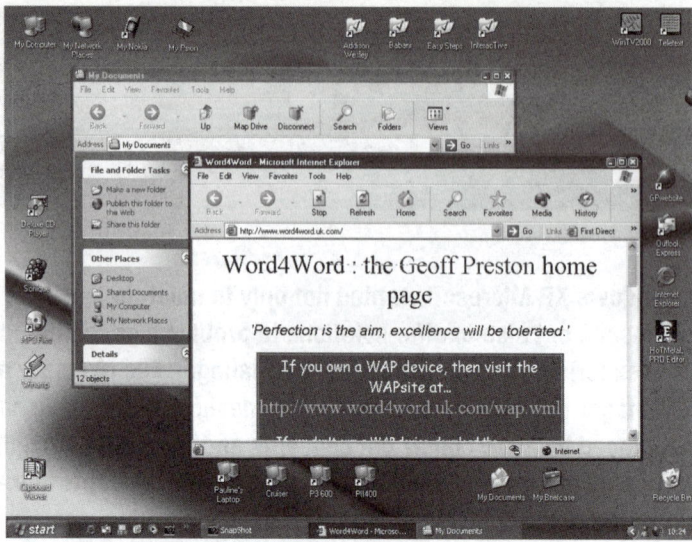

Figure 3.1 The Windows XP Desktop, with two windows open.

You will see three types of object (Figure 3.1): the icons, the Start button (at the bottom left of your screen) and the Taskbar (along the bottom of your screen). One of the items shown on our bar is the Snapshot button, which is the program that was used to create the screenshots for this book. The bar in our example also features My Computer and Explorer, which represent the windows open on the Desktop.

Timesaver tip

Taskbar and Switch To function The Taskbar replaces the Switch To function of Windows 3.1. The new method is infinitely more practical. However, the Switch To facility can still be accessed by pressing the key combination **Alt + Tab**.

The Taskbar allows you to:

- use the Start button and run a program
- open the window of a program waiting in the background (e.g. Snapshot)
- swap from one task to another (i.e. from one program to another, or from one window to another).

The My Computer icon provides an overview of your PC. It is more logical and easier to take on board than in earlier versions of Windows. Double-click on the **My Computer** icon on the Desktop to open it.

The My Computer window displays the hard disk drive and CD-ROM drive and the Control Panel folder (Figure 3.2).

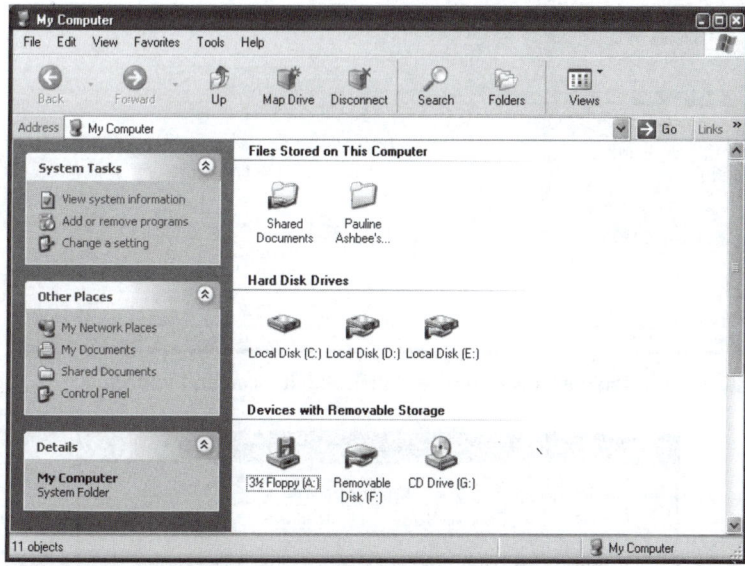

Figure 3.2 My Computer, a logical and global view of the PC.

By double-clicking on [C:], you can open the contents of the hard disk (Figure 3.3). Each directory is represented by a folder and any files entered in the hard disk drive are shown.

→ My Computer properties

In Windows XP, each object shown on the Desktop has properties that can easily be looked up or modified. Right-click on the **My Computer** icon. This brings up a 'context-sensitive menu' that allows you to open My Computer or activate its properties. Click on **Properties** to open the System Properties dialog (Figure 3.4). Click on the relevant tab to display the properties you are interested in: General, Computer Name, Hardware, Advanced, Automatic Updates, Remote and System Restore.

Discovering the interface 23

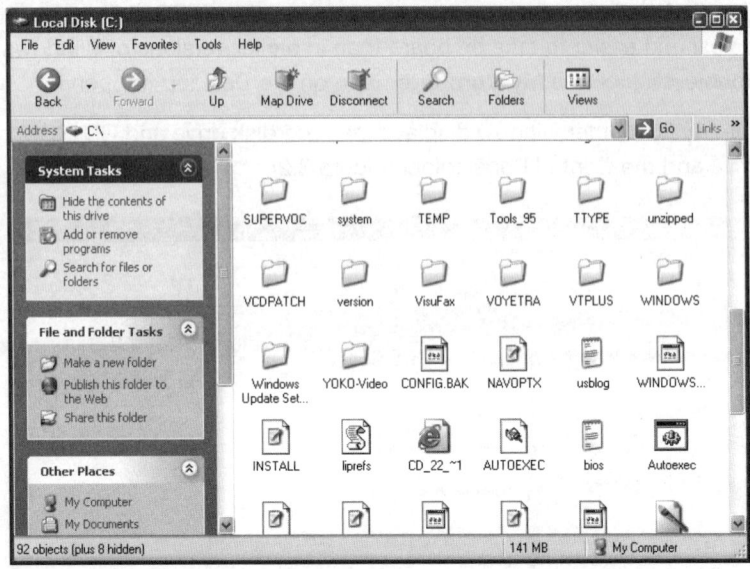

Figure 3.3 A logical view of the hard disk with its files and folders.

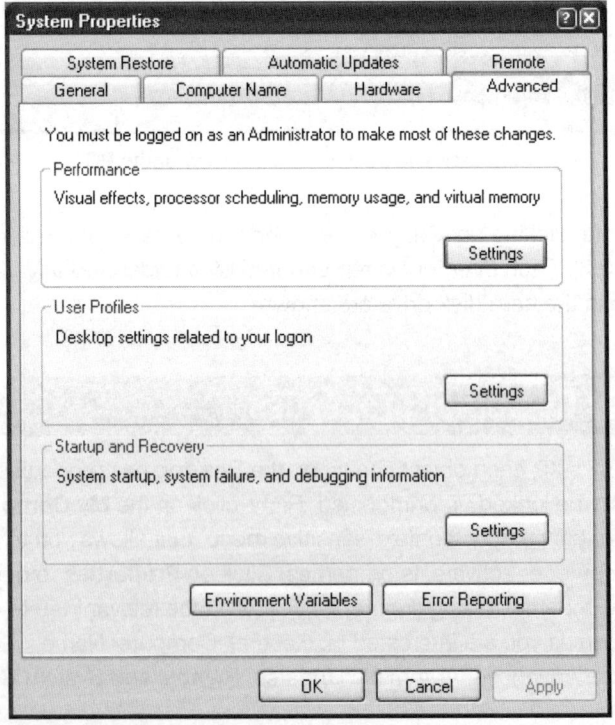

Figure 3.4 The System Properties dialog.

24 Brilliant Microsoft® Windows XP Pocket Book

Figure 3.5 The Device Manager dialog.

Click on the **Hardware** tab and then **Device Manager** button. The Device Manager dialog (Figure 3.5) is used to examine the hardware configuration in precise detail. It is structured hierarchically: level one, or the root, represents the PC itself, while the second level brings together the major device families, shown according to hardware type.

Information

The hardware profile The PC or computer you are working with is described by a hardware profile. Once you have installed Windows XP, a default hardware profile is created, which collates all the technical characteristics of your machine. You can also create other profiles that can be activated at will when you start Windows. While this facility is of limited use to the beginner, it can be implemented at corporate level when the same PC is used under different conditions, i.e. by more than one user.

The + sign to the left of each device means that the equipment in question may be detailed and comprises subsets. Click on the + sign to open out the tree structure. You can see a drop-down list of the system devices. The list shows individual components, such as the disk drives, the mouse, and the keyboard configuration.

Inexperienced users need not concern themselves with all this technical information. It is mainly to enable advanced users to examine their PCs in meticulous detail and to make any necessary changes. Double-clicking on any hardware component in the tree structure brings up a display of the technical characteristics of that component. The Properties button provides information on equipment operation, parameter assignments (settings), the resources deployed (in this case, the driver) and any hardware conflicts detected.

The Advanced tab of the System Properties dialog (Figure 3.4) provides information on the performance of your computer. From the basic information supplied, you will see the percentage of system resources used. Other parameters relating to disk optimization (File System), Virtual Memory management or display optimization (Graphics) may be used by experienced users or corporate system administrators.

We will discuss object properties in more detail later. The example chosen here, although somewhat technical, shows how easy it is to obtain information on your working environment (in this case, the computer). At this stage, we shall confine ourselves to pointing out that the object properties procedure applies to all object families: an object can be the PC hard disk, a local network, a program or a document.

→ The Taskbar

The Taskbar is very important. It serves as the control tower for your workbench. Its chief aims are to help you in your work and to speed up the transition from one program to another or, to be more accurate, from one task to another.

The Taskbar was designed to meet day-to-day requirements, i.e. starting applications, finding documents, moving from one task to the next, and so on. The Taskbar is split into parts (from left to right) (Figure 3.6):

Figure 3.6 The Taskbar.

- the Start button
- the Quick Launch bar (see Chapter 7)
- a list of active tasks
- a series of system settings icons.

The right-hand side of the Taskbar contains icons that give access to volume control, display parameters, scheduled tasks (see Chapter 11), and the date and time properties.

→ The Start button

The Start button is your real contact point in Windows XP. Click on it to display a menu giving access to programs and documents using Windows, or major commands such as shutting down the operating system (Figure 3.7).

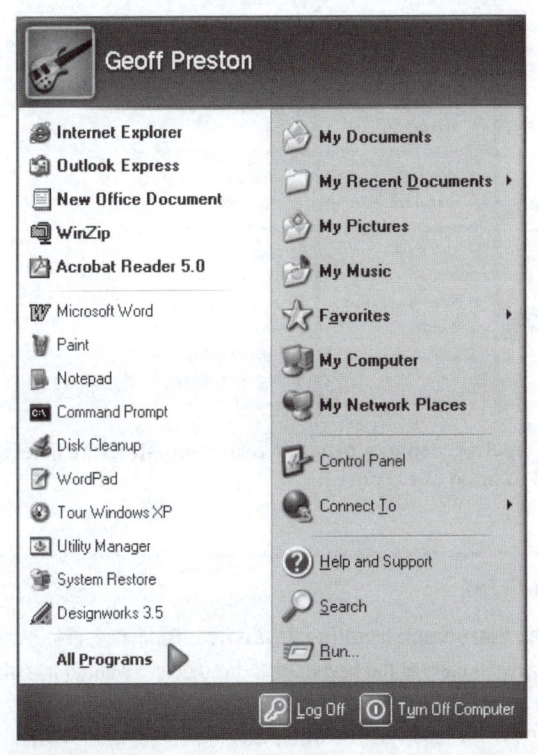

Figure 3.7 The Start menu.

Discovering the interface

The small arrow to the right of certain parts of the menu means that there is a submenu for that option. Simply point to the selected menu with the mouse to display details. In Figure 3.8 we have scrolled through the All Programs, Accessories and Communications menus in turn.

Figure 3.8 Direct access to a program using tree-structure lists: simply click on an object to open or execute it.

Timesaver tip

Opening the Start menu from the keyboard For convenience, when you are busy typing text at the keyboard and you do not want to use the mouse, you can activate the Start button by pressing the Windows key (the one with the flying window) or the **Ctrl + Esc** key combination. Hit **Esc** to close the Start menu.

28 Brilliant Microsoft® Windows XP Pocket Book

With the Start button you no longer need to conduct time-consuming searches among different groups of programs. Nor is there any need to double-click on the icon of the program you wish to run (as you have to in Windows 3.1). The Start button gives you faster access to a program or document. It also does away with the 'program' aspect of the Windows 3.1 interface since, from the Start button, the Documents menu gives direct access to the last documents used.

Timesaver tip

Windows Update will link you to Microsoft's Web site to update your copy of Windows XP with the latest developments.

→ Smart menus

The Windows XP Start menu is a smart menu! It is designed to respond to the way you work, displaying at first only the core items and those that you use regularly (Figure 3.9) – once it knows which they are. The rest are tucked out of sight, but can be revealed either by waiting a few moments or by clicking on the double-arrow bar at the bottom of the menu. If you use a program, it will be added to the menu and become part of the displayed set in future. If you don't use a program for several days, it will be dropped from the menu. As smart menus are normally much shorter, it makes selection simpler and faster.

Information

Manipulating windows When you run a program, it opens an application window that you can close again by clicking on the X symbol at the top right corner of the window; you can expand (maximize) or contract (minimize) it by clicking on the underscore symbol (_). When the window is minimized, its icon can be seen on the Taskbar – restart it by clicking on it. This operating mode applies to any type of window (Figure 3.10).

Discovering the interface   29

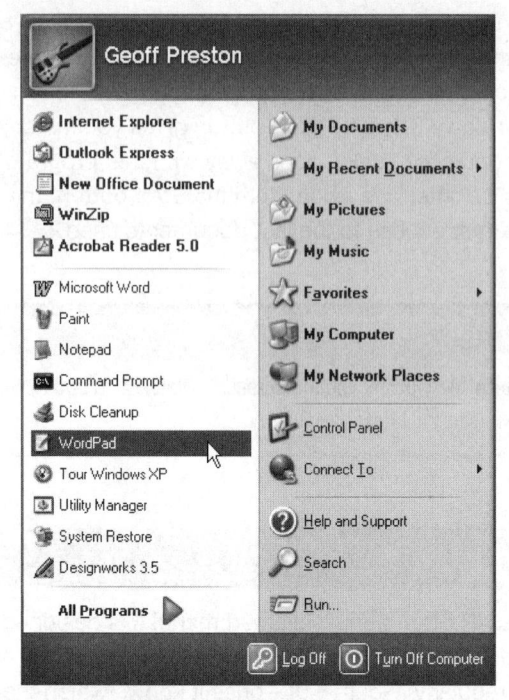

Figure 3.9 The Windows XP Start menu will respond to the way you work.

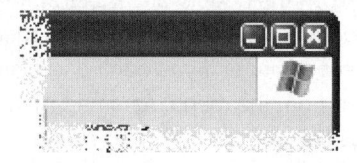

Figure 3.10 The three buttons on the top right of a window.

The Programs menu

The Programs menu contains the most frequently used applications. To run a program, simply select it and click. This list of programs, and all other lists accessed from the Start button, can be customized, as we shall soon discover.

The Documents menu

The Documents menu under the Start button lists the last 15 documents used and gives direct access to the My Documents (and My Pictures) folders. A simple click brings back a document you recently worked on, irrespective of the program in which it was created. Remember that a document can be text, a spreadsheet, a graphics image, a photograph, a sound file or even a video clip.

The Search menu

The Search menu (Figure 3.11) under the Start button is used to find a program or a file; to find a PC in a local area network, or a document or service on the Web; or even to find individuals on the Net. The features offered here are considerably more powerful than those offered by the old File Manager, while their extension to the Internet greatly increases their usefulness.

What do you want to search for?

- Pictures, music, or video
- Documents (word processing, spreadsheet, etc.)
- All files and folders
- Computers or people
- Information in Help and Support Center

You may also want to...

- Search the Internet
- Change preferences

Figure 3.11 The Search menu.

To find a file or folder, click **Files and Folders**. The Search Results window will open (Figure 3.12). This is actually My Computer (see Chapter 4) with the Explorer Bar set to Search mode.

A simple search can be by all or part of the filename or for some text within a file – or a combination of the two. Suppose, for example, you were trying to find a letter about tax but could not remember what you called it or where you stored it. You at least know that it contained 'tax' and that it was a *Word* document – and so would have the .doc extension. You could simply give 'tax' as the name, and the search would find it, but if you gave 'doc' in the filename slot it would speed up as the search would then only have to read through document files (plus any others that happened to have 'doc' somewhere in their names) and could ignore all the rest.

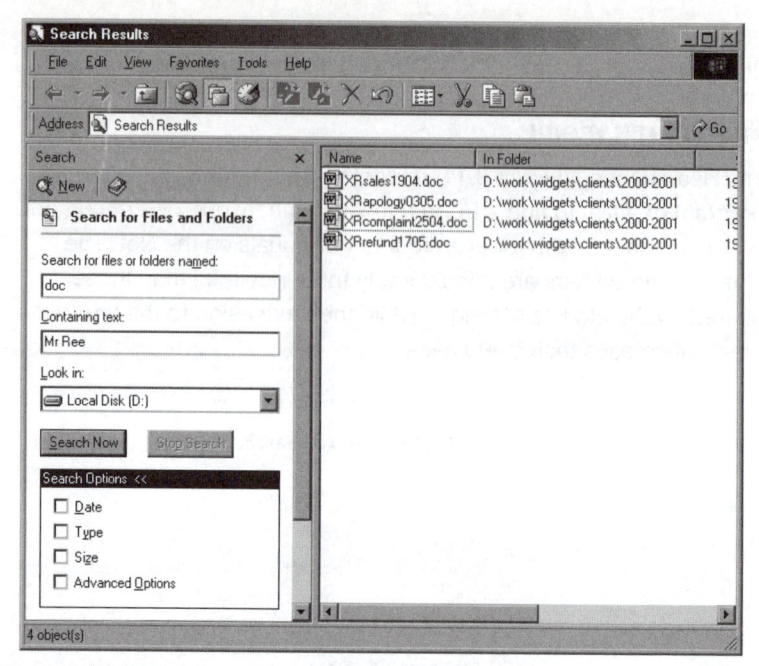

Figure 3.12 Search by name and by containing text.

Timesaver tip

Find by contents The Containing text box enables you to conduct a search based on specific contents. Hence, in a set of signed documents, you can carry out your search based on the signature or keywords of your choice. You can also find on your PC all the files that contain certain groups of words.

You can speed up the search further by specifying which drives or folders to start looking in. Note that the search will normally look into all the subfolders below the start point.

Click **Search Now** to start the search. It may take a few moments.

In the Search Options area you can define a search by specifying Date, Type, Size or Advanced Options. If you know when a file was created, modified or last accessed, you can set the date limits. The little drop-down calendar provides a very neat way to set dates! The type can be picked from the long drop-down list. Specifying the size might be useful sometimes. The Advanced Options are rarely much use. They simply let you turn off the subfolder search or turn on case sensitivity.

The file search by name facility uses a character string that may contain the wildcard characters '?' and '*'. Here are a few examples:

- **Mode**: find all objects containing the letters 'mode'.
- **M?de**: the '?' can replace any character.
- **Mo*e**: the '*' character can replace any string of characters between 'Mo' and 'e'.

Figure 3.13 shows a typical search pattern, displaying details of the files found. The result may be displayed in one of five ways: Tiles, Icons, List, Details or Thumbnails. These options are available by clicking on the **View** tab.

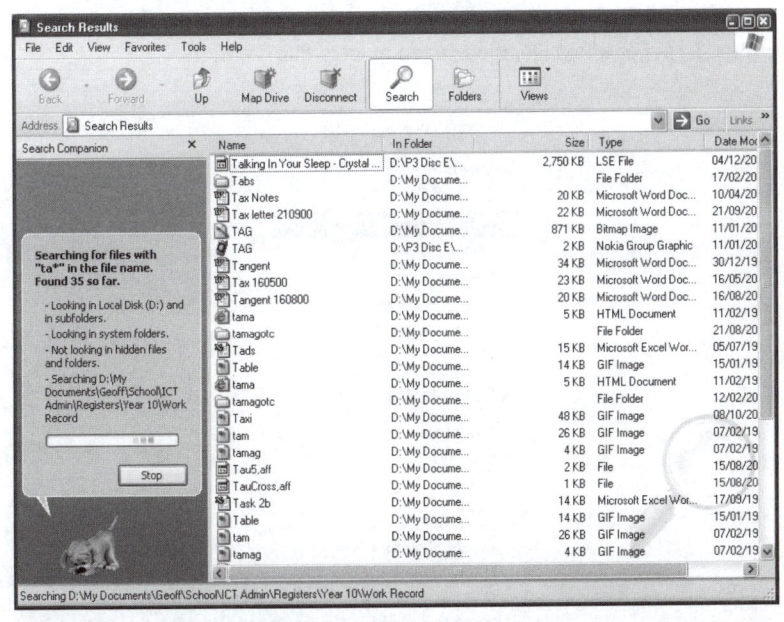

Figure 3.13 Using the options to define a search.

Right-click on the **File** tab for a range of options that change according to the nature of the object selected. Thus, in the case of a text file, the menu offers alternatives such as Print or Send To (Figure 3.14). In the case of a folder, an Explore option or a fresh Search within the same folder are offered (Figure 3.15).

Windows XP deploys the principles of dynamic processing, depending on the properties of the objects you wish to find. In the file tab, some options are common to all objects, while others are dependent on the type of object:

Discovering the interface 33

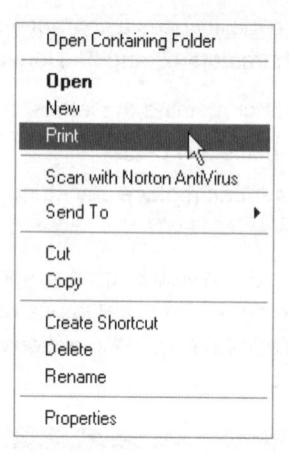

```
Open Containing Folder
Open
New
Print
Scan with Norton AntiVirus
Send To                    ▶
Cut
Copy
Create Shortcut
Delete
Rename
Properties
```

Figure 3.14 For a text file, the File tab reveals this menu …

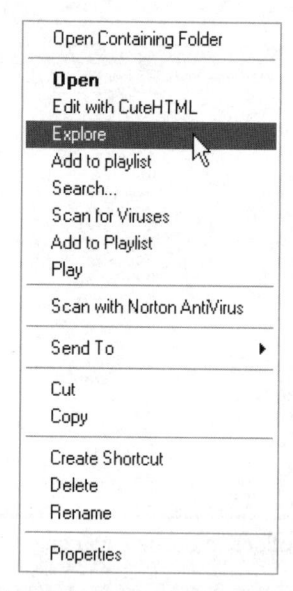

```
Open Containing Folder
Open
Edit with CuteHTML
Explore
Add to playlist
Search...
Scan for Viruses
Add to Playlist
Play
Scan with Norton AntiVirus
Send To                    ▶
Cut
Copy
Create Shortcut
Delete
Rename
Properties
```

Figure 3.15 … for a folder, the File tab reveals this menu.

- **Open**. Opens a document or starts the selected program or, if the object is a folder, opens a My Computer window to display its contents. We will deal with this utility in the next chapter.

- **Open with**. When the nature of the selected object is not identified, Windows XP sets out a list of programs that might be able to open the selected file.

- **Print**. Prints a text file directly.

- **Play**. Plays a sound file immediately. To do this, Windows XP uses the Media Player, which is supplied as standard. At the same time, a video clip will be displayed in an independent play window.
- **Explorer**. Uses a folder file to start up Windows XP Explorer. We will deal with this utility at a later stage.
- **Find**. If the selected object in the resulting list is a folder, this option opens a new search window.
- **Send To**. This is a particularly powerful communications option, which we will also discuss in detail at a later stage. Three despatch options are offered: a fax addressee, a message addressee, and a diskette. If your PC is equipped with a fax/modem facility, mail can be sent directly in this way. Instructions are given by the Compose New Fax Wizard.
- **Delete** and **Rename**. Delete sends the object to the Recycle Bin, which we will describe later. Rename lets you do just that.
- **Properties**. Looks up the object's properties.
- **Create Shortcut**. Provides a quick method for accessing the object at another time.

Timesaver tip

Stopping a search   The Stop button allows you to suspend processing at any time. This is useful if the processing seems to be taking too much time, especially if the file sought has just been added to the results list.

The Help menu

The Help menu under the Start button opens the Windows XP Help facility. Online Help operates like hypertext language used on the Web: one click and you obtain links to another explanation, other programs or wizards.

The Run menu

The Run menu is used to run a program directly when you know its name. If you cannot remember its name, press the **Browse** button to search the Desktop or work from My Computer.

You will find that this command also allows you to open an Internet site or Web page address.

Discovering the interface   35

The Shut Down menu

You know how to start Windows XP, but you also need to know how to shut it down. To access the Shut Down menu, click **Start**, **Shut Down**. The Shut Down menu offers you a number of options (Figure 3.16):

- Hibernate (shut down, but not log off). When restarted, the computer will be as you left it, including open programs and folders.
- Total system shut down.
- Shut down with immediate restart.

Figure 3.16 Shutting down Windows XP.

> **Timesaver tip**
>
> **Change of user on a PC**   The Log off submenu, which can be accessed from the Start menu, closes down all active applications and opens a new working session. If you choose this option, Windows XP invites you to enter a new user name and password, so connection is re-established under a different working environment.

> **Timesaver tip**
>
> **Stopping a task without shutting down Windows XP**   Pressing the **Ctrl+Alt+Del** keys simultaneously in Windows 3.1 was irrevocable and forced you to restart the PC. In Windows XP, you can use this key combination to halt a current task and carry out the necessary backup procedures; these are displayed in a dialog.

The Taskbar and Start menu

Right-click on the Taskbar and choose **Properties** from the menu to open a dialog (Figure 3.17).

If the Keep the taskbar on top of other windows option is deactivated, the Taskbar may disappear or be partly obscured by a working window.

If the Auto-hide option is activated, the Taskbar disappears from the Windows XP Desktop. It remains active, however: simply drag the mouse pointer to the bottom of the screen to slowly bring it back into view. If you put the cursor back on to the Desktop, the Taskbar will drop down again and disappear.

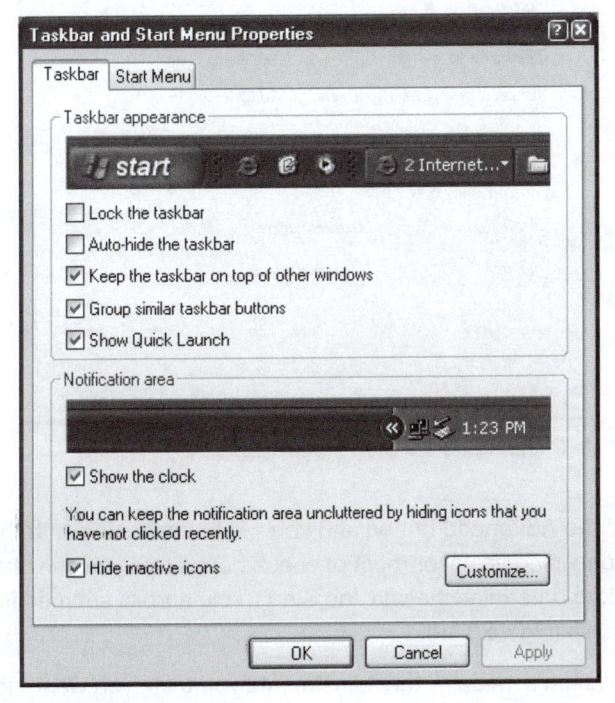

Figure 3.17 Windows XP Taskbar and Start menu settings.

A particularly useful feature is the Show Quick Launch icons, which provide a number of buttons for commonly used programs.

You can also decide to display smaller icons under the Start button, and to show the time on the right-hand side of the Taskbar.

Discovering the interface 37

Start menu settings

Now let's customize the Start menu. Click on the **Start** menu tab in the Properties dialog and choose the **Customize** option. Here you can choose either large or small icons and select the number of program icons you want to appear on the left of the Start menu (Figure 3.18).

Figure 3.18 Customizing the Start menu.

Click on the **Advanced** button and you will be presented with three areas containing an assortment of check boxes that you can check or uncheck to determine the way the Start menu and its submenus look and behave (Figure 3.19).

When you have made all the adjustments you think you want for the present, click **OK**. You can, of course, return to the dialog to make further adjustments, including undoing some you have just made.

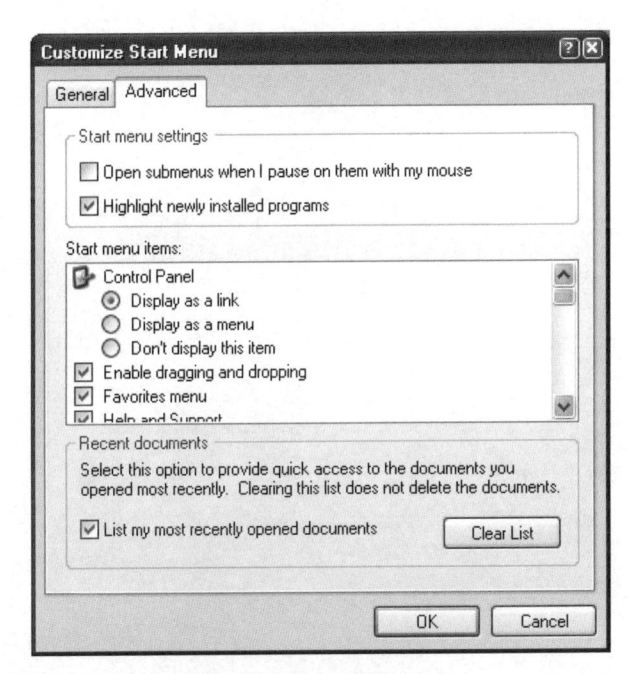

Figure 3.19 The Advanced customizing settings.

4 Working in Windows XP

Working on a daily basis in Windows XP requires familiarity with a certain number of operations (shortcuts) and tools (the Explorer).

→ Changing from one task to another

The Taskbar enables you to change easily from one task to another, from one program to another or from one document to another. The Windows XP user is a true 'screen hopper' with the ability to keep several jobs (windows) active simultaneously. The role of the Taskbar is to ensure a smooth transition.

This bar, conventionally positioned at the bottom of the screen, can actually be relocated to any part of the screen. As various applications are activated, it shows all the buttons for the relevant active programs. These buttons are scaled down so that they can all fit on the Taskbar (Figure 4.1).

Figure 4.1 The Taskbar.

Multiple versions of similar active tasks will appear as a number on the Taskbar button. For example, '4 Internet Explorer' means that Internet Explorer has four active versions. Clicking on the Taskbar button will open a menu listing the versions, which may be displaying different pages.

In our example in Figure 4.2, Paint has been started first, followed by My Documents, Microsoft Word, WordPad and Media Player. WordPad and Media Player are open and Media Player is active. A CD is playing.

In Figure 4.3, the Media Player window has been minimized by clicking on the ■ symbol at the top right corner of the window. The task remains active and you can listen to music at the same time as running the Windows XP WordPad program.

Figure 4.2 The Desktop with two applications open, one of which is active.

Figure 4.3 The Desktop with a job in progress in WordPad while simultaneously listening to music.

Next, all the windows have been minimized, again by clicking on ■ at the top right of the window (Figure 4.4). To activate them again, click the relevant program button on the Taskbar. When you minimize a task

42 Brilliant Microsoft® Windows XP Pocket Book

by clicking on ■, a fast, animated image shows the window being reduced until it takes the form of a Taskbar button.

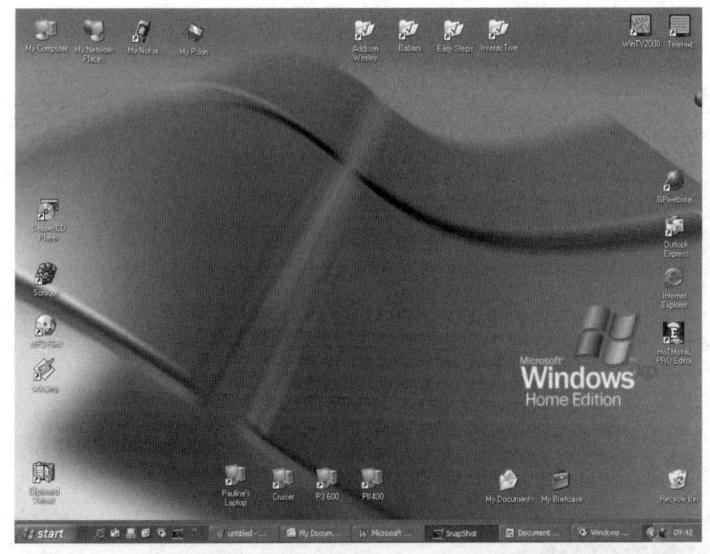

![Figure 4.4 screenshot of Windows XP desktop]

Figure 4.4 You can activate the program of your choice from the Taskbar.

> **Timesaver tip**
>
> **Finding out the properties of objects on the Taskbar** By clicking the right-hand button of the mouse on free areas of the Taskbar, you can call up the properties of objects and adjust them accordingly.

Conversely, reactivating a task restores the size of the button to the initial size of the working window.

The number of buttons on the Taskbar is the same as the number of active tasks. Buttons are automatically resized so that they all fit on the bar. For improved legibility, you can increase the size of the Taskbar by dragging its upper edge with the mouse.

→ The Recycle Bin

Windows XP Recycle Bin is used to get rid of objects (folders, programs, text documents, images, etc.). In Figure 4.4, the Recycle Bin is visible at the bottom right of the Desktop. To dump a file, simply click and drag the object in question to the Recycle Bin icon. Alternatively, right-click on the object you want to send to the Recycle Bin, then click on **Delete**. To delete several objects at a time, hold down **Ctrl**, select all the objects to be deleted, right-click, then click on **Delete**.

If you make a mistake, you can open the Recycle Bin by double-clicking on its icon (Figure 4.5). Point the mouse to the items you wish to retrieve and then press the right button: click **Restore** to correct the mistake. The Delete option in this menu is irreversible, unless you have a dedicated retrieval utility (undelete or unerase) on the disk. If you want to retrieve the entire contents of the Recycle Bin, you can activate the Restore option in the **File** tab. To empty the bin, use the Empty Recycle Bin option (Figure 4.6). If a confirm option has been set (it exists as a default), you will receive a final message asking you whether you really do want to empty the Recycle Bin.

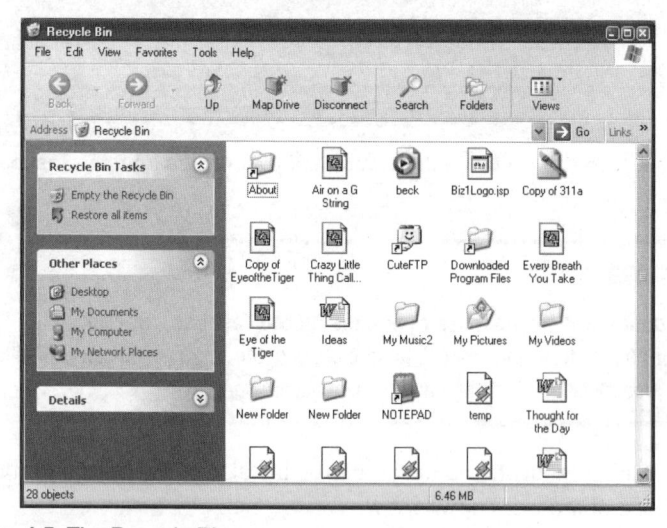

Figure 4.5 The Recycle Bin.

Figure 4.6 **Empty Recycle Bin** irrevocably deletes the files from your hard disk.

→ Starting a program

Several methods are available for starting a program that is not currently active. These methods show the versatility of Windows XP:

- Click on **Start**, **Run**.
- Click on **Start**, **Programs**, then click on the program of your choice.
- Double-click the **My Computer** icon, and scroll through the hard disk contents [C:]. Position the cursor over the name of the program you want to open, then double-click. Alternatively, right-click on the name of the program and click **Open**.
- Use the Search option in the Start menu to locate the program.
- Open Explorer, find the application, then double-click on its name.
- If you have a shortcut to the program on the Desktop, double-click on the shortcut icon.

We can see from this example how the Desktop, My Computer and Start button provide resources for organizing your work to suit your personal needs.

My Computer

In the My Computer menu (accessed from the Windows XP Desktop), a disk or folder can be opened by double-clicking on it or, after selecting it with the right-hand button of the mouse, by activating the Open command. This calls up a window that displays the relevant files and folders as large, easily readable default icons.

Experienced users can reconfigure the display mode if they wish. Open **My Computer**, then click on the **View** tab. Choose one of the five display modes from the menu (Figure 4.7):

- Thumbnails
- Tiles
- Icons
- List
- Details (size of file, update time, etc.).

Thumbnails shows a miniature image of the document, if possible. This option is not always available.

We shall learn how to use the Explorer Bar command in Chapter 9.

```
Toolbars          ▶
✓ Status Bar
  Explorer Bar    ▶

  Thumbnails
  Tiles
• Icons
  List
  Details

  Arrange Icons by ▶

  Choose Details...
  Go To           ▶
  Refresh
```

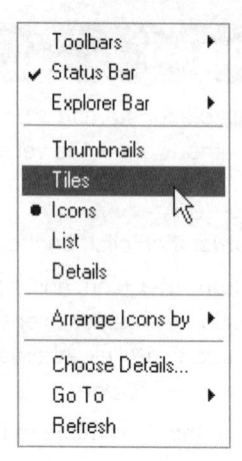

Figure 4.7 My Computer View Options.

The default display mode uses icons that are easier to read and easier to control than lists of files. This display method is also used in Windows 95 and 98. Lists will be appreciated by more advanced users, while icons are likely to appeal to new users. An icon might, for example, represent a folder that can be opened by double-clicking on it, or by clicking the right-hand mouse button and selecting Open.

The View menu also lets you activate the toolbars. In the View menu, click on **Toolbars**:

- **Standard Buttons**. This bar gives access to basic functions (parent buttons to go up the tree structure, cut-and-paste functions, deleting an object, etc.).
- **Address Bar**. This bar allows you to type in a file location on the hard disk or, as we shall see later, a Web address.
- **Radio**. Use this to listen to radio on the Internet when you are online.
- **Customize**. This option lets you add buttons to and remove them from the toolbar. You can also turn text labels for the button on or off here.

Handling files and folders

Files and folders can be handled very easily and moved around using the mouse. Right-clicking on a file brings up a menu (Figure 4.8) that allows you to cut, copy, paste, rename or delete the file.

> **Information**
>
> **File names** The limit on the size of file names in Windows 3.1 (eight characters, plus a three-character extension) was a legacy of DOS. With Windows XP, as with Windows 95 and 98, you can use extended file names (up to 255 characters). You do not need to type in an extension, as the relevant extension for the file type is handled automatically by the program in which the file has been created.

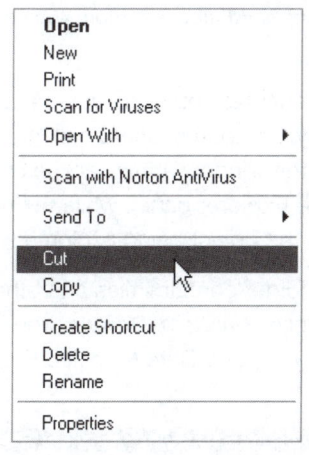

```
Open
New
Print
Scan for Viruses
Open With              ▶
Scan with Norton AntiVirus
Send To                ▶
Cut
Copy
Create Shortcut
Delete
Rename
Properties
```

Figure 4.8 File operations.

→ Managing objects with Explorer

Windows XP Explorer is the program you use to navigate folders and files. Explorer provides an overall view of the PC's environment. All local disk resources (My Computer), as well as the disks that can be accessed via a network (My Network Places), are displayed on the same level. Explorer can also find documents on the Internet. This unique presentation simplifies life for the user.

Windows XP Explorer can be called up in a number of ways:

- Click on **Start**, **Programs**, **Windows Explorer**.
- Right-click on the **My Computer** icon, then click **Explore** (Figure 4.9).

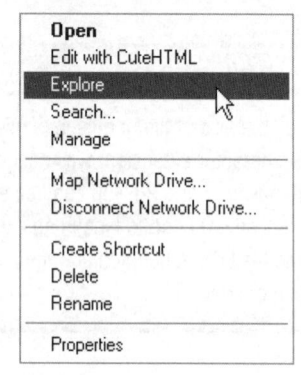

```
Open
Edit with CuteHTML
Explore
Search...
Manage

Map Network Drive...
Disconnect Network Drive...

Create Shortcut
Delete
Rename

Properties
```

Figure 4.9 Using the right-hand mouse button, you can activate the Explorer option.

Windows XP Explorer enables you to determine the contents of an object, whether it is My Computer, a hard disk or a folder (Figure 4.10). The left-hand pane of the window shows all the objects in the environment (this is the Explorer pane), while the right-hand pane shows the contents of the object being explored.

Generally speaking, a folder contains files and other folders. To sort your folders and files, click on **View**, **Details**. You will see four columns: Name, Size, Type and Date Modified (Figure 4.10). Decide

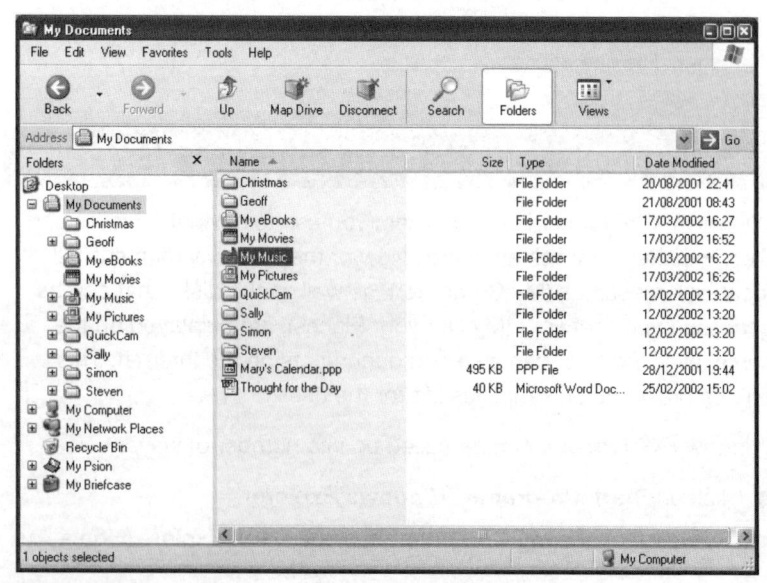

Figure 4.10 The contents of a folder in Explorer.

48 Brilliant Microsoft® Windows XP Pocket Book

how you want to sort your objects, then click on the relevant column heading. Clicking on the same heading reverses the sort direction.

To create a new object (e.g. a folder, shortcut, text file, WordPad document, image or sound), point the mouse at a free area to the right of the contents, click the right-hand button, and click on **New**. Select the type of object you want. A new icon appears in the window; you then simply give it a name.

→ Properties of objects

All objects handled in Windows XP have properties that you can look up at any time, simply by right-clicking the mouse to activate the Properties command. You can find this feature in the Properties screen of My Computer. Several dialogs will be offered and you can change from one page to the next by clicking the relevant tabs.

The information supplied in the hard disk Properties box will, of course, be quite different. The space available on the disk is displayed in the General dialog as a graphic (Figure 4.11). The Tools menu offers two options:

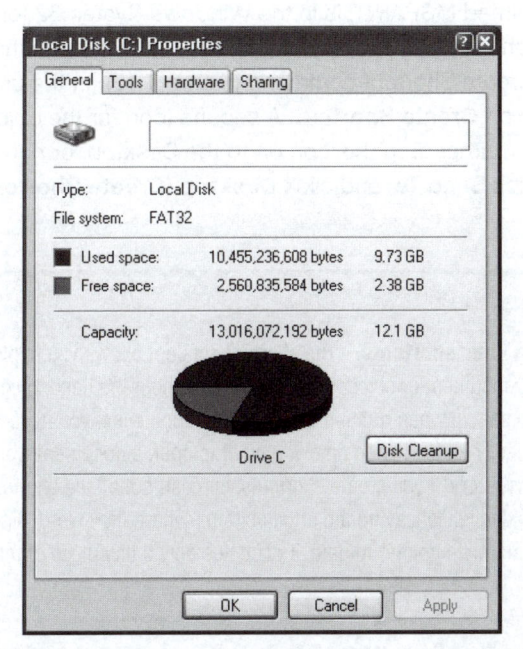

Figure 4.11 Displaying the properties requested for the hard disk.

- ScanDisk, for checking for disk errors
- a disk defragmenter.

These two programs are part of the System Tools facility that can be found from the Start menu (see Chapter 11).

→ Shortcuts: the fast way to fetch an object

Shortcuts are powerful links that will enhance your productivity in Windows XP. You can create a shortcut to any type of object – a file, program, folder or even the hard disk. Even better, you can put the shortcut where you want on the PC, even in a document. When you open a shortcut, the object it is pointing to is automatically activated. Shortcuts are displayed in the same way as any icon: they represent the image of the object they are pointing to. They are distinguished by a small folded arrow at the bottom left of the icon.

For our example, we will create a shortcut to the program Paint. This can be called up from the Start menu but, as we have several screenshots to do, we would like to access it from the Desktop. A search (Find) will enable us to find this program on the disk: the program, named MSPAINT, is in the Windows System32 folder. From Explorer, right-click on this object. The drop-down menu that appears offers the Create Shortcut command (Figure 4.12). In the drop-down menu, click on **Create Shortcut**. A second icon for the object will appear. Now either drag the icon on to the Desktop, or right-click on the icon, click **Send To**, and click **Desktop (Create Shortcut)**.

> **Timesaver tip**
>
> **Organizing your shortcuts**   The shortcut concept allows you to place an application, document or object in several files without the need to copy them. For instance, when running a multimedia application you need to delve into a number of folders. Each time you want to open a document, you have to change directory. If you create shortcuts, you can put all the shortcuts in the same folder, while leaving the original items where they were. Since the shortcut is merely a pointer to data, it occupies only a tiny piece of memory (255 bytes).

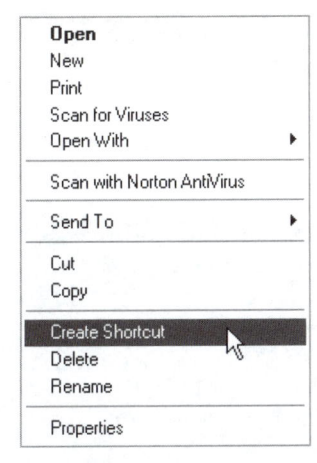

```
Open
New
Print
Scan for Viruses
Open With                    ▶

Scan with Norton AntiVirus
Send To                      ▶

Cut
Copy

Create Shortcut
Delete
Rename

Properties
```

Figure 4.12 Creating a shortcut.

Shortcuts can be moved to any location: to the Desktop, the Start menu, or the My Computer icon. It's up to you! The most frequently used programs could be placed under the Start button along with key documents, while you could position the disk drives or shared network resources with, for example, current business on the Desktop.

Timesaver tip

Placing a shortcut in the Start menu To do this, drag the shortcut icon to the Start button. The shortcut will then automatically position itself in the main menu under this button, from where you can then run the programs you use most often without having to worry about where to find them.

→ Customizing the Start menu

Right-click on the **Start** button and choose **Properties** from the menu to open the Taskbar and Start Menu Properties dialog. Click the **Start** menu tab and choose **Customize**. In the new dialog, select the Advanced tab (Figure 4.13). At this stage, you are able to reorganize this menu completely by means of cut-and-paste or add operations. You can also drag a Desktop object to the Start menu.

Figure 4.13 Selecting programs in the Start menu.

New shortcuts can be created directly by clicking on **File**, **Create Shortcut**. Existing shortcuts can be moved, copied or deleted in the Explorer window, or even placed in this window from the Desktop (drag and drop with the mouse).

→ Handling diskettes

The disk drive can be accessed from My Computer. If the drive is used frequently, you can create a shortcut on the Desktop to read a diskette quickly.

The diskette is opened by double-clicking on the [A:] icon, or by right-clicking the icon, then clicking **Open**. This menu also allows you access to the diskette formatting and copying commands (Figure 4.14).

Timesaver tip

Copying files To copy a PC file to diskette, simply drag and drop it with the mouse. Alternatively, right-click on the file's icon, click on **Send To**, then click **3½ Floppy [A:]**. Similarly, you can drag and drop one or more files from the diskette to a folder in the PC.

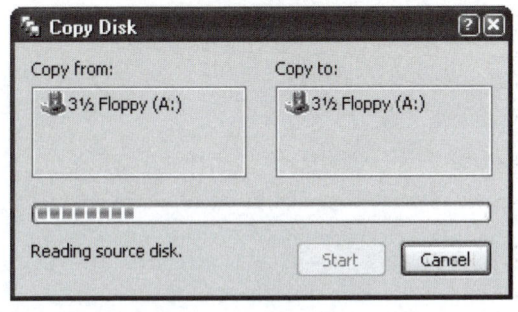

Figure 4.14 Copying a diskette.

5 The Control Panel

→ The Control Panel

At installation, Windows XP will have optimized your system and set parameters for the individual components. You can use the Control Panel to look up settings, improve them and adapt them as your environment changes. Thus you can change your password, modify your monitor display settings or even install a new modem. The Control Panel (Figure 5.1) can be accessed from the Start menu.

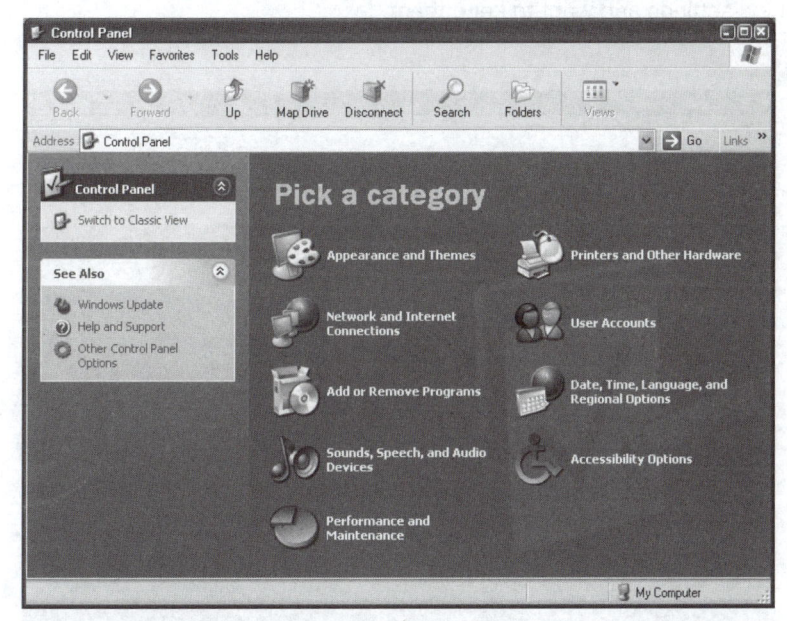

Figure 5.1 The Windows XP Control Panel.

Many configuration options are accompanied by wizards to assist you. Wizards take the hard work out of installing new peripherals, thanks to plug-and-play technology.

→ Accessibility options

The accessibility settings enable you to tailor Windows to your own particular working environment. This is especially useful for new users, and also for users with physical disabilities, as special settings have been created to suit special needs.

In the Control Panel, click on **Accessibility Options**. There are three options available:

- Adjust the contrast for text and colours on your screen.
- Configure Windows to work for your vision, hearing and mobility needs.
- Accessibility options.

The first and last options lead to a dialog (Figure 5.2) while the second option takes the form of a wizard. For all settings proposed, click **Apply** to try out the individual settings or **OK** if you are happy with the new settings and want to keep them.

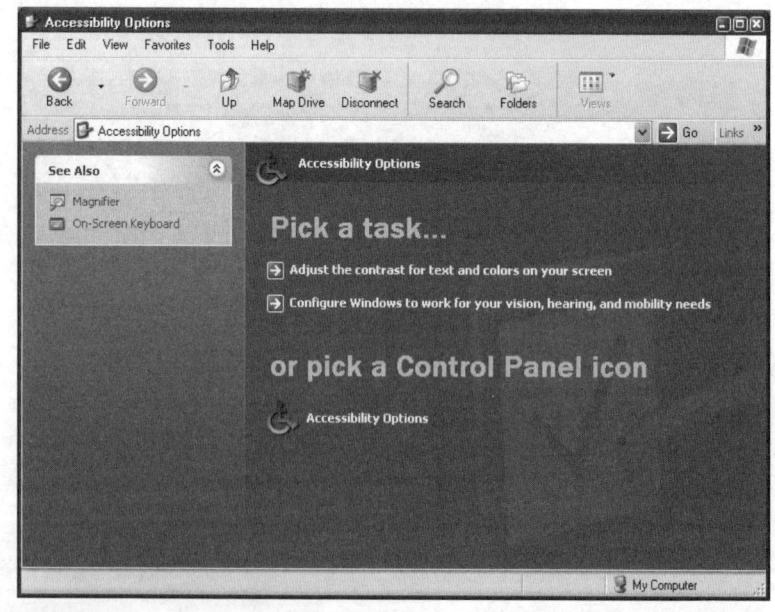

Figure 5.2 Accessibilty Options.

56 Brilliant Microsoft® Windows XP Pocket Book

Keyboard set-up

The Keyboard tab enables you to set up the keyboard. It offers three setting modes:

- StickyKeys
- FilterKeys
- ToggleKeys.

To activate one of these modes, tick the appropriate **Use ...** box, then click on the **Settings** button to specify the key settings.

> **Timesaver tip**
>
> **StickyKeys** StickyKeys is ideal for people who find it difficult to press two keys at the same time. With this setting, you can apply the Shift, Ctrl or Alt key simply by hitting the key once followed by the next key – you don't have to keep your finger on the Shift, Ctrl or Alt key when you hit the next key. For example, to type a capital letter, you would hit Shift and then the relevant character key, rather than hitting them both at the same time.

The FilterKeys setting overrides accidental or repeated keystrokes.

The ToggleKeys function instructs the PC to generate a high-pitched sound when you press Caps Lock, Scroll Lock or Num Lock, or a low-pitched sound when you deactivate one of those keys.

> **Information**
>
> **Mouse set-up** The mouse settings tab enables you to use the four arrow keys on the numerical keypad to move the cursor, to click and double-click, and even to drag objects. The settings screen allows you to define a shortcut key to switch this function off and to adjust the pointer speed.

Sound and picture settings

The Sound tab in the Accessibility Options dialog (Figure 5.3) is used to link an image or text to a sound message in Windows XP. People who are hard of hearing appreciate this option. Two features are offered. You can use SoundSentry to show a flashing sign on the

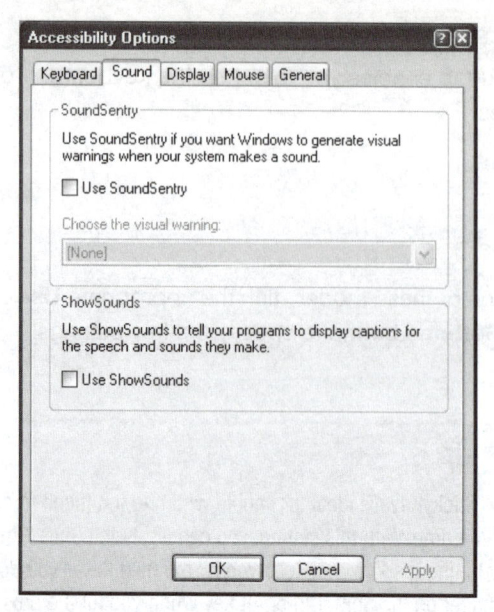

Figure 5.3 Linking an image or text to a sound message.

screen for each sound generated by the PC. The area that flashes can be designated by clicking on the **Settings** button. Alternatively, use ShowSounds to display written captions instead of sounds.

You can also adjust the monitor display and select colours or fonts that are easier to read. To do this, click the **Display** tab, the **Use High Contrast** box, and click the **Settings** button.

→ Monitor display settings

In the Control Panel, click on **Appearance and Themes**. The Display Properties dialog lets you change the appearance of your screen. The Desktop tab lets you set the background for the Desktop (Figure 5.4). You can pick a wallpaper in bitmap format (.BMP), which is then applied to the Desktop. By clicking on the **Browse** button, you can find a .BMP file on the hard disk and assign it to the Windows XP screen background.

The Screen Saver tab is used to set up a screen saver.

The Appearance tab (Figure 5.5) enables you to set interface colours (screen background, window title bar, control button, etc.) based on a given specimen.

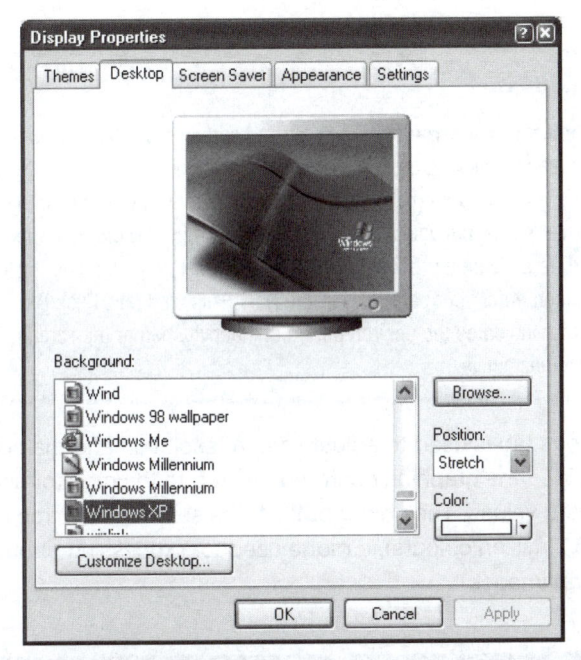

Figure 5.4 Changing the background.

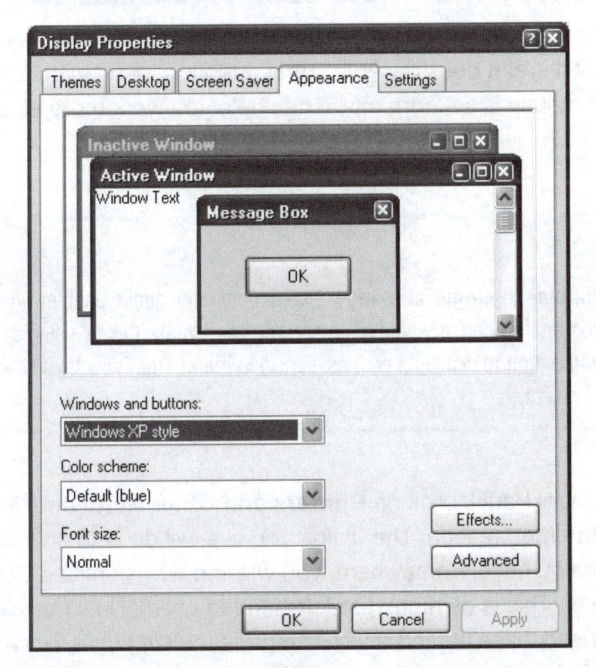

Figure 5.5 Desktop appearance settings.

> **Timesaver tip**
>
> **Testing screen saver mode** The selected screen saver can be viewed on the full screen by clicking on the **Preview** button. You can also protect your PC by means of a password. When your system is on standby, the animated screen saver starts, but your PC can only be used again by entering the password. To activate a password, tick the Password Protected box, click on **Change**, then enter your password in the New Password box. Click **OK**. The Wait counter indicates the desired period of inactivity before the screen saver becomes active.

The Settings tab is used to adjust screen resolution and the colour box, provided the graphics board connected to the monitor accepts the selected values. The colour box can be set to 32-bit 'true colour' mode (16.7 million colours), a mode used for processing photographs and bitmap images.

→ Mouse set-up

The mouse is so familiar to most users that it seems unnecessary to talk about it. Yet it does deserve some attention, particularly since once the mouse is set correctly, it can help you work more efficiently in Windows XP.

> **Timesaver tip**
>
> **From double- to single-clicking** The double-click action enables you to run a program or open any type of object. You can bypass this by using the right-hand button to display a context-sensitive menu, from which you can open the object.

In the Control Panel, click on **Printers and Other Hardware**. Then choose the **Mouse** icon. The dialog you see will depend on what sort of mouse you have. Somewhere, you will find a box entitled Buttons (Figure 5.6). This is of interest to left-handed users. Until now, left-handed users have battled away, using the middle finger for selecting options and the index finger to obtain the context-sensitive menu (which allows you to access the properties of objects); now you can change the rules of the game. Simply click the left-handed option in the Button configuration menu.

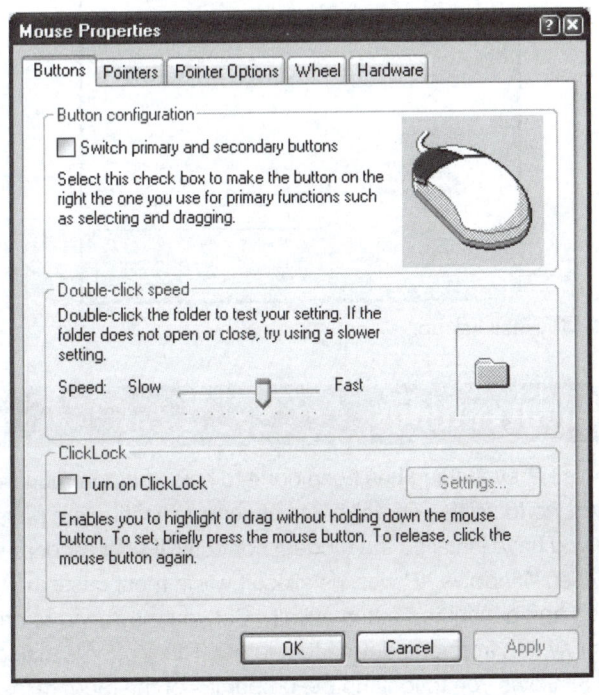

Figure 5.6 Left-handed use of the mouse.

→ Joystick set-up

A few years ago, joysticks were not very sophisticated; today, there are a number of models adapted to a range of games software: flying a fighter plane, driving an F1 racing car, etc. Broomstick, multi-axis spinners, multibutton controllers, rudders – there are many variants of games devices. The Game Controllers dialog, accessed from the Control Panel (Figure 5.7), enables you to select your equipment and set it up properly. It is simply not possible to indulge in aerial stunts without the correct broomstick settings.

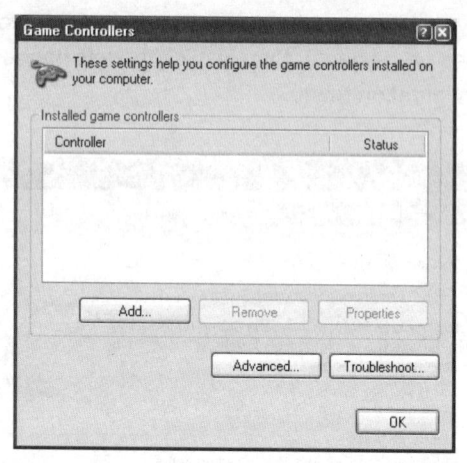

Figure 5.7 Joystick set-up.

→ Modem settings

In Windows XP, everything has been done to help you communicate with the outside world. With a PC, all types of communication are possible, provided you have installed the modem correctly. If your modem was present when Windows XP was installed, it will in most cases have been recognized and configured automatically. But you may need to enter new settings or switch from one device to another. The Modems dialog (Figure 5.8) allows you to look up the properties of the modem installed.

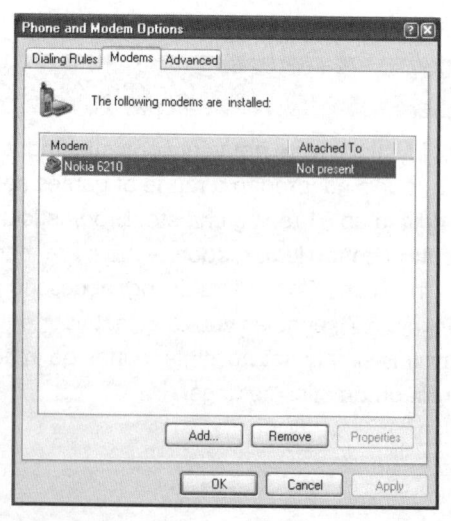

Figure 5.8 Properties of the modem installed.

→ Date and time management

It is important that the date and time in your PC are set correctly. This enables you to program events (downloading on the Internet, PC monitoring) and to store your documents with the correct details (such as the date of last modification). You should also set the time zone by clicking directly on the map displayed, or selecting a region in the world from the drop-down list.

> **Timesaver tip**
>
> **Setting the time** You can display the date and time properties by clicking directly on the time displayed on the right-hand side of the Taskbar. Use the Date/Time Properties dialog to modify the date and time.

→ Sound management

It is possible to link a sound to a Windows XP event. Nearly 30 events (Windows start-up, Program error, Opening a window, Receiving new mail, etc.) can be set in this way for amusement or operational reasons. For example, you might link a sound to create battery run-down alerts for portable PCs (Figure 5.9).

When Windows XP is installed, the sound board is automatically detected and is referenced as a peripheral by default. By ticking the Show volume control box, you can alter the setting directly from the Taskbar.

These sounds or audible messages are .WAV format files. If you have a sound board and a microphone, you can record your own messages with the Sound Recorder (**Start**, **Programs**, **Accessories**, **Entertainment**, **Sound Recorder**).

→ Multimedia set-up

The sounds, speech and Audio Devices link in the Control Panel provides you with all the sound, music and video settings required. The Audio tab (Figure 5.10) controls the sound board volume.

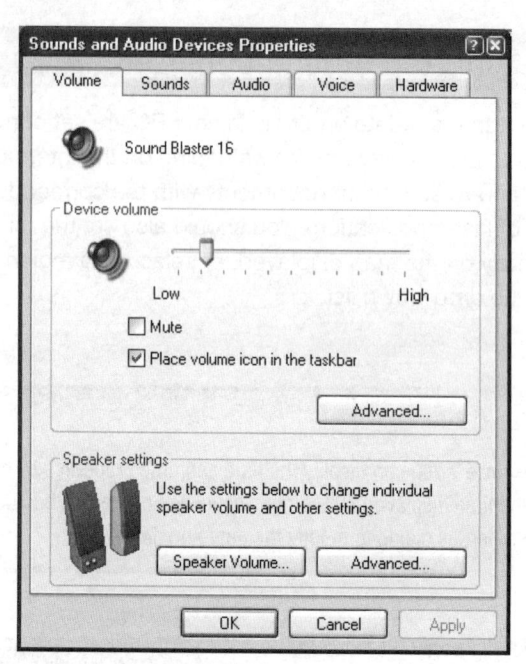

Figure 5.9 Sound settings.

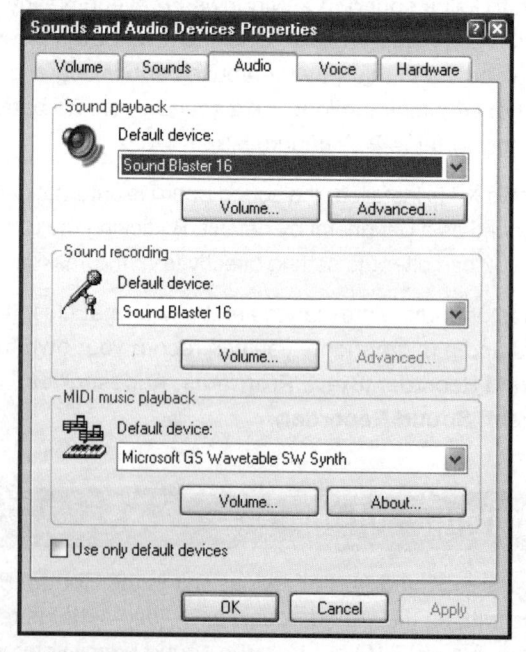

Figure 5.10 PC Audio settings.

The same screen allows you to set the recording level if you have a microphone or other type of audio input device and wish to record files in .WAV format.

In the Advanced Properties box, a drop-down menu enables you to select the required quality: the higher the quality, the larger the sound file will be. A number of recording quality levels are offered and can be adjusted using the cursor. The best quality offered is equivalent to that provided by an audio CD.

Timesaver tip

Listening to audio CDs on your PC If your CD-ROM drive incorporates a headphone socket, you will be able, via the software, to set the volume level for listening to audio CDs.

→ Printer management

The Printers and Other Hardware link (Figure 5.11) in the Control Panel allows you to call up printer and fax settings, provided you have installed a fax board or module in your PC.

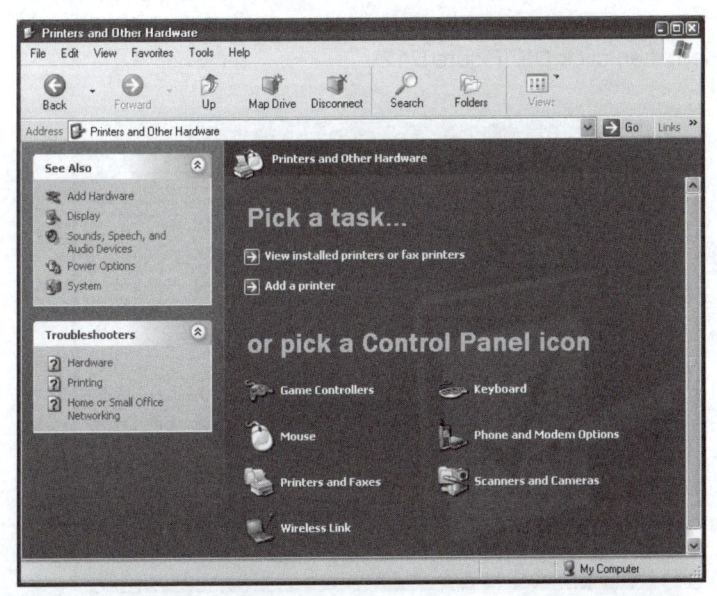

Figure 5.11 The Printers Control Panel.

> **Timesaver tip**
>
> **Opening the Printers folder**   The folder can also be opened directly from the **Start**, **Settings** menu.

From here you can set up a printer or install a new one. By clicking **Add a printer**, you activate the Add Printer Wizard. You can choose the make and model and specify the connection port. You can decide whether this printer is to be the software default printer. On completion of the installation process, the wizard invites you to run a print test. This enables you to check that the printer is working properly.

→ Font management

From the Control Panel, choose **Appearance and Themes** and then click the **Fonts** link on the left of the window to provide access to all the typographical styles stored in your PC.

When you open a Fonts file, it gives you information on the font in question and you can display the characters in different modes and sizes. The Print button gives you a hard-copy sample of all the possible variants based on that font (list of characters, character size, etc.). To add a font, click **File**, **Install New Font**. Select the font to be added, then click **OK** (Figure 5.12).

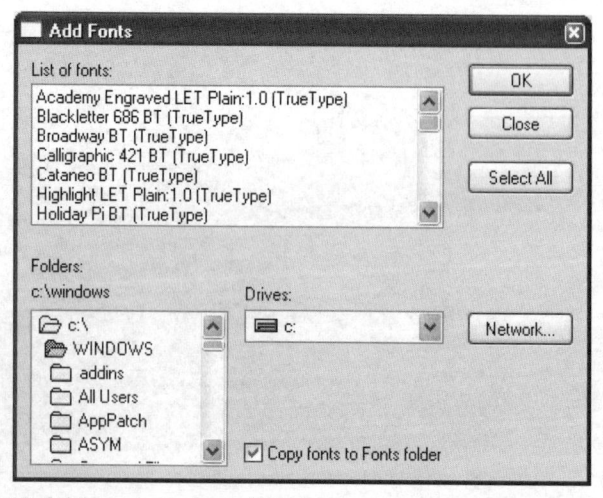

Figure 5.12 Adding one or more fonts.

→ Mail management

The Mail settings can be used to create new Internet mail accounts, if these are not created as part of the installation routines when you set up your connection to your Internet Service Provider. Click the **Add** button to start the wizard, then respond to its prompts to supply the details of your mail service.

Windows XP also has its own fax software, which allows you to send and receive faxes on your PC.

→ Connecting to the Internet

Select **Network and Internet Connections** from the Control Panel and choose **Internet Options** to open a dialog, which allows you to check your Internet connection and, if necessary, to modify its settings. You can use the Internet Connection Wizard to specify an initial (or new) connection to an Internet Service Provider (Figure 5.13). The wizard may be accessed by clicking on the **Connections** tab on the dialog and choosing **Add** (Figure 5.14).

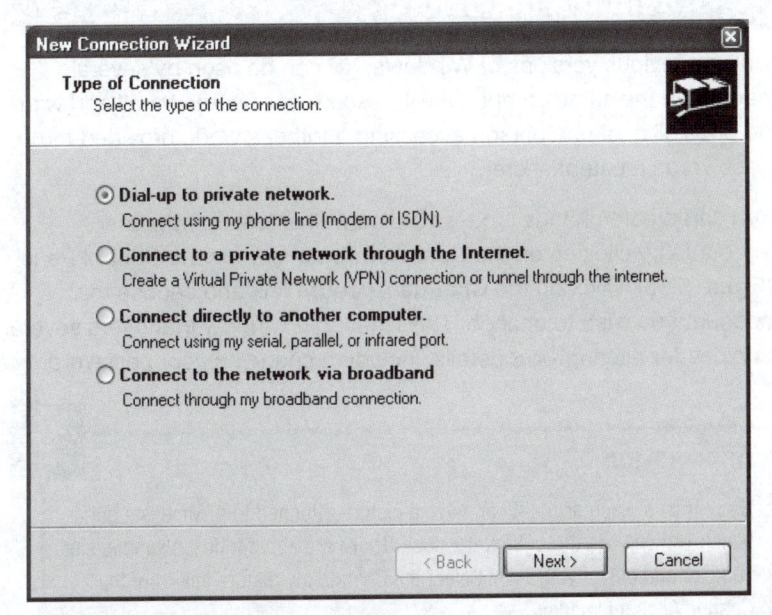

Figure 5.13 The Internet Accounts Wizard.

The Control Panel

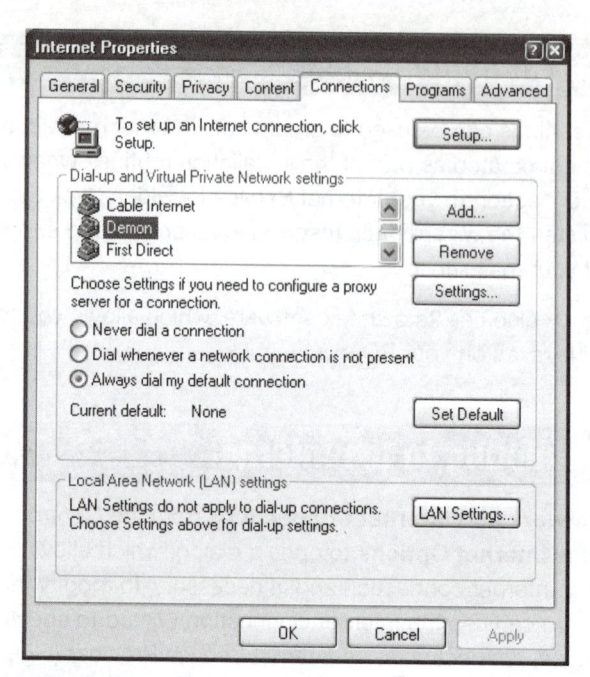

Figure 5.14 The Internet Properties dialog.

→ Creating a password

Unlike previous versions of Windows, XP can be used by several people on the same computer, with secure passwords for all and with no possibility of one person accessing another's work, provided the passwords are kept secret.

You can create/change a password as well as create new user accounts by clicking on the **User Accounts** icon on the Control Panel (Figure 5.15). Click on the **Change Account** link and choose the account you wish to change. This leads to a window that offers several choices for altering your details, including changing your password.

Information

User icons Each account can have a picture attached to it. Mine is a guitar, which you will see throughout the book. There are about a dozen supplied, or you can add one of your own. Select the Change my picture link from the Change Account window.

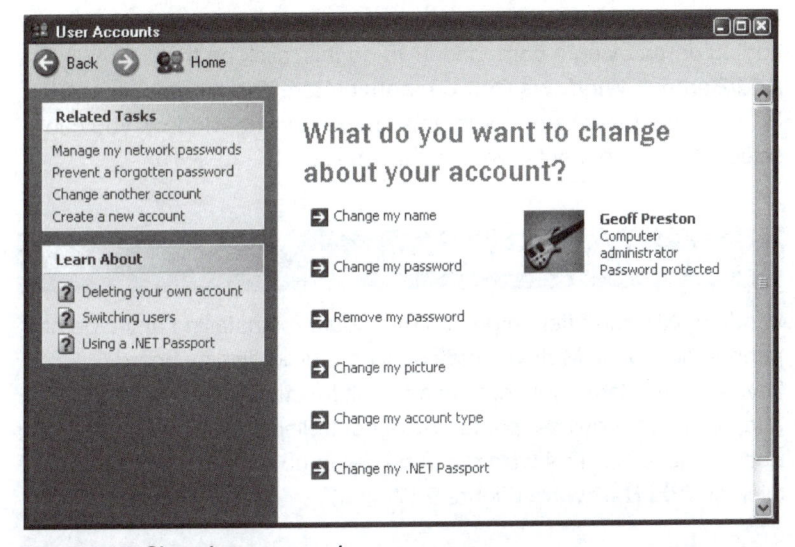

Figure 5.15 Changing passwords.

→ Adding applications

From the Control Panel, select the **Add/Remove Programs** icon. From this dialog, you can install (or uninstall) programs from the floppy disk or CD-ROM drive. Click on the **Add New Programs** button, then choose the appropriate source (Figure 5.16).

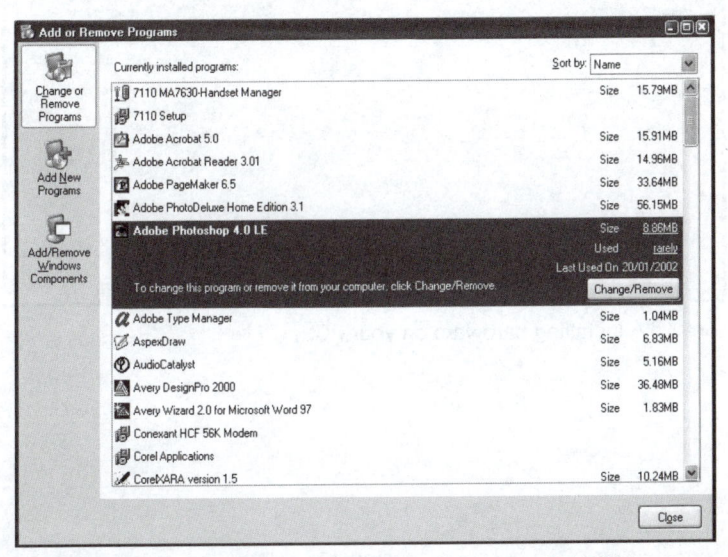

Figure 5.16 Installing a new program from a diskette or CD-ROM.

The Control Panel 69

As well as installing applications, you can fine-tune Windows XP by adding or removing a component. To do this, click on the **Add/Remove Windows Components** button. The program scans the PC to detect the resident programs. In the working window, you can select new components, or uninstall others.

→ The Add Hardware Wizard

Windows XP also offers a guided procedure for installing any type of peripheral: CD-ROM drive, additional hard disk, display board, keyboard, modem, mouse, monitor, multifunction board, network adapter, PCMIA device, printer, SCSI controller, sound board, digitizing board or joystick. This wizard can be called up from the Control Panel: click on **Add Hardware** (Figure 5.17).

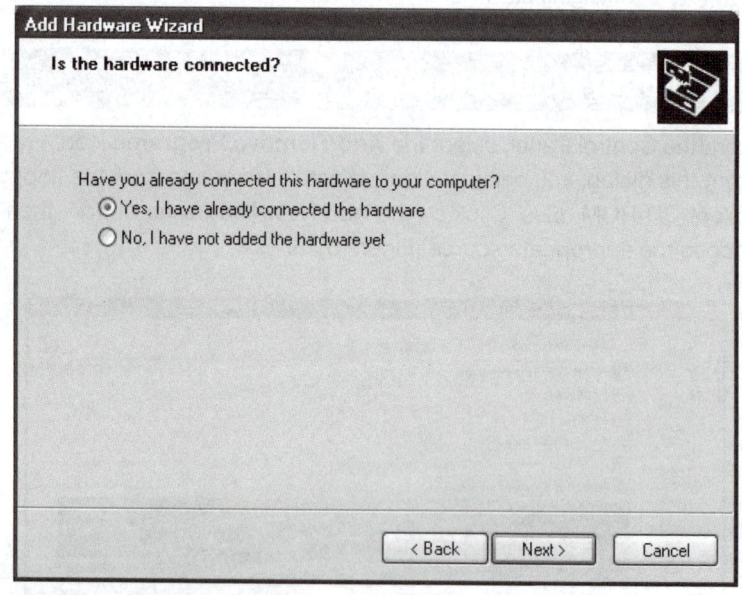

Figure 5.17 Installing hardware on your PC.

6 Windows XP tools

Windows XP contains all the accessories that were included with Windows 98. These can be called up from the Start button by selecting **All Programs** and then **Accessories**.

→ The Calculator

The Windows XP calculator can operate in standard or scientific mode. To toggle from one to the other, simply select the type of calculator required in the View menu.

→ Notepad

Notepad provides a highly practical way of displaying a text file (Figure 6.1) or entering text quickly.

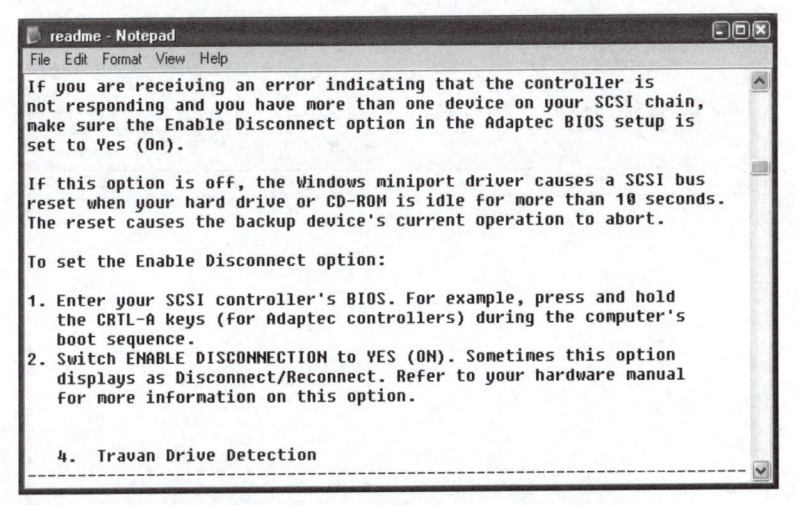

Figure 6.1 The Windows Tips and Tricks file opened with Notepad.

> **Timesaver tip**
>
> **Date your activities in Notepad** You can create a dated log using Notepad. To do this, simply enter the command '.LOG' on the first line of the document, in the left-hand margin. Then save the file. When you call it up at a later stage, it opens with the current date and time at the end of the text. This enables you to keep a list of activity dates on a particular topic.

→ Word-processing in WordPad

If the Notepad facility does not meet your needs for inputting and editing text documents, you can use WordPad, a 32-bit word-processing program supplied as standard with Windows XP.

WordPad (Figure 6.2) is an extremely powerful word-processing package, with a highly functional interface. Texts entered or retrieved in WordPad can be saved in the following formats (using the **Save** command in the File menu):

- text only (.txt)
- RTF format, useful for exchanges with Macintosh computers (.rtf)
- Word for Windows format (.doc).

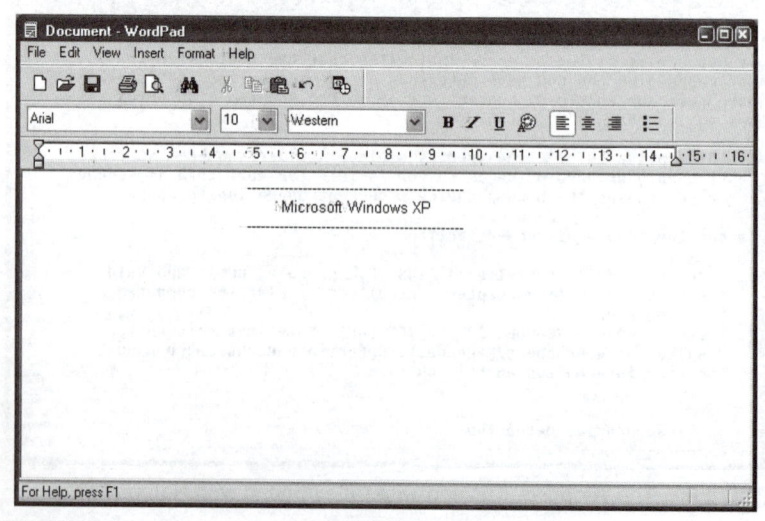

Figure 6.2 Word-processing in WordPad.

72 Brilliant Microsoft® Windows XP Pocket Book

> **Timesaver tip**
>
> **Inserting multimedia objects in WordPad** The Insert menu allows you to insert objects in a document. WordPad supports OLE 2.0 technology (object linking and embedding) for incorporating objects. This enables you to use the functions of another application in WordPad and to create genuine multimedia documents.

→ The Paint program

Windows XP is supplied with Paint, a bitmap drawing software package that enables you to create customized background pictures for the Windows Desktop, or to prepare images to be inserted in WordPad documents.

From the File menu, you can ask for the image to be applied as wallpaper for the Windows XP Desktop, either tiled or centred.

The Paint software incorporates a toolbox, a colour box and a status bar. These areas may be closed down from the View menu. The toolbox offers all the conventional drawing functions (Figure 6.3).

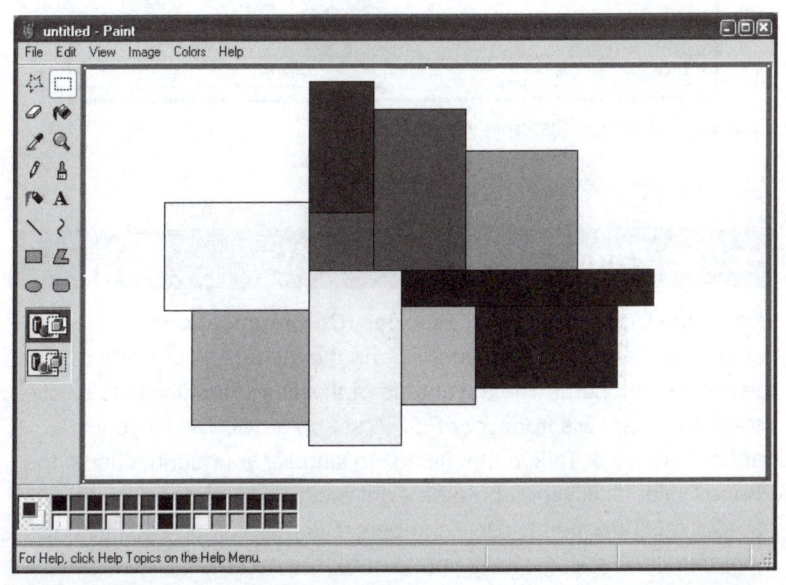

Figure 6.3 Some modern art using Paint.

> **Timesaver tip**
>
> **Special effects** The Image menu allows you to work on the selected portion of the image. For example, with Flip/Rotate you can rotate the selected zone horizontally or vertically, or you can choose a particular angle. You can also invert colours: this gives you a negative of the image.

The Colors menu (Figure 6.4) brings up the colour-handling functions. The menu enables you to define a set of customized colours. The palette you create can be saved and then used again later.

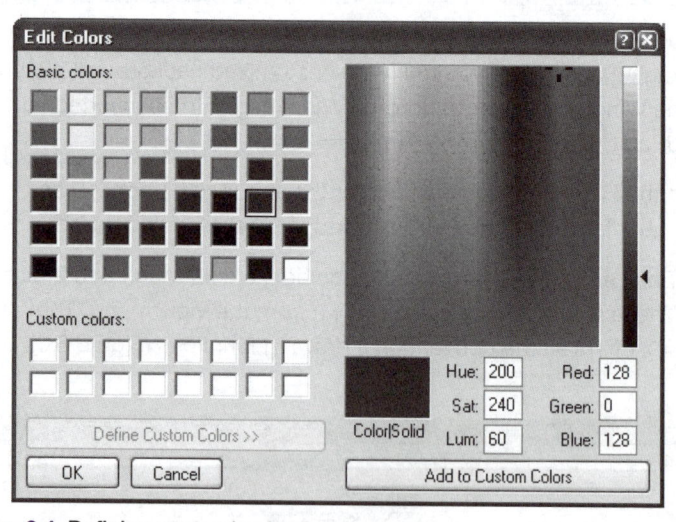

Figure 6.4 Defining customized colours.

→ The Phone Dialer

The Phone Dialer facility (**Accessories**, **Communications**) is used to set up telephone calls from your PC via the modem or any other telephone peripheral. The advantage of this lies in the ability to easily establish voice calls from your PC. To set up a call, you lift your handset and click **Talk** in the dialog. To simplify your connections, the Phone Dialer facility incorporates eight memory locations (Speed dial) for your most frequently used numbers. Simply click on each field to store details. A dialog allows you to enter the names of correspondents and their telephone numbers.

→ Character Map

There are many characters that cannot be easily accessed using the conventional keyboard. Character Map (Figure 6.5) displays all of the characters in a convenient grid and allows you to copy and paste individual characters or groups of characters into another document.

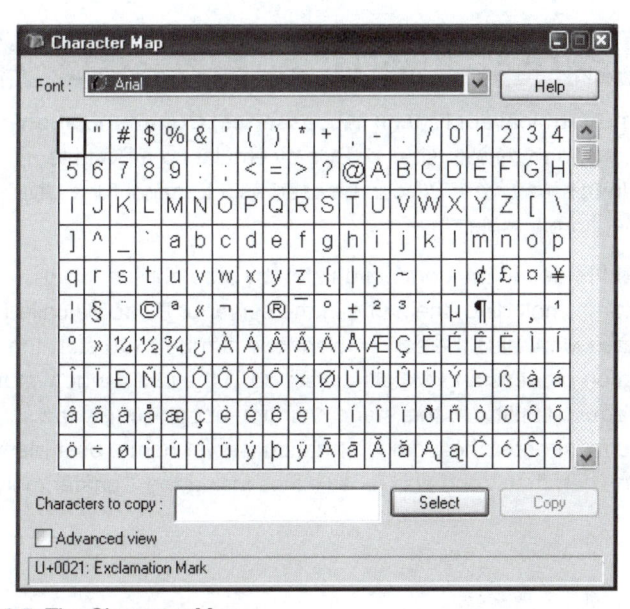

Figure 6.5 The Character Map.

Begin by selecting the font style from the drop-down list at the top of the dialog and then click on the character you wish to use. Click the **Copy** button to make a copy, which can then be pasted into another document (e.g. WordPad). If you wish to use several characters, click the **Select** button after each choice. You can then click the **Copy** button to copy all the chosen characters.

This is a simple and convenient way of entering characters which are peculiar to languages other than English – those with accents (Ä, è, ê, ö, ß), for example, and for symbols such as degrees (°) and copyright (©).

→ Remote Desktop Connection

This useful program enables you to connect to a remote desktop (or for others to connect to your desktop) so that you can help, or be given help, to move files between desktops and generally interact with another Windows user.

→ The HyperTerminal utility

The HyperTerminal application (**Accessories**, **Communications**) connects you to remote sites or PCs by emulating a PC in terminal mode. In this way, your PC can be used as a terminal for a UNIX machine, for example.

You need to define the connection step by step (for the initial connection), including the name of the server or PC to be called and the related icon, plus the server telephone number. You start the connection process and a dialog is set up in the text window of the HyperTerminal utility. At this stage, you are recognized by the server and you must enter the login information (server name, user identifier, etc.). You can then send and receive files (using the Transfer menu).

7 Windows XP and the Internet

→ The Start button

Everything begins here in Windows XP. When you click on the Start button, you immediately find the user Log Off function (Figure 7.1). This is a useful feature in offices where a PC is shared among a number of people. At the end of a working session, you can log off without shutting down Windows. The next user can start the system using his or her own custom settings.

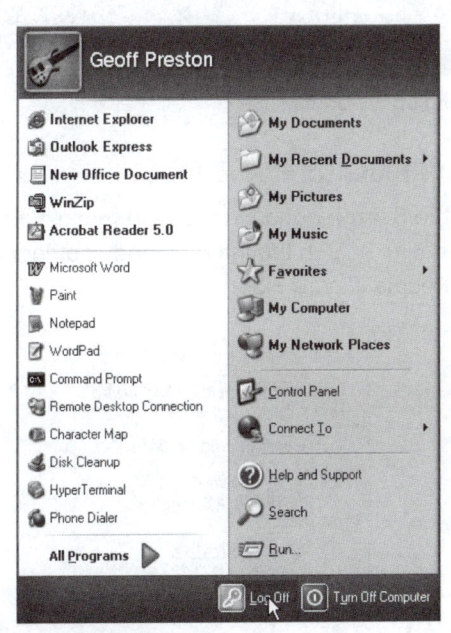

Figure 7.1 The user Log Off function.

Calling up favourite Web sites

From the Start button, you can access your favourite Web sites. Click **Favorites** to call up your personal list of Web sites (Figure 7.2).

The contents of this menu will soon change as you start to add your own favourites. Initially it will contain some links set up for you. These will include:

- recommended sites, generally determined in collaboration with your PC manufacturer
- technical links to the Microsoft site
- connection to the Microsoft site to update your Windows software.

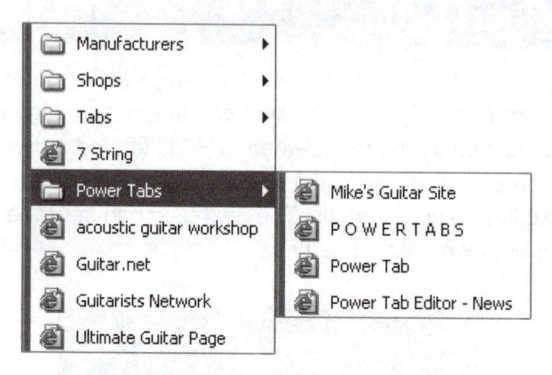

Figure 7.2 Calling up Favorites.

Finding documents on the Web

If you click on the **Search** option in the Start menu, you will see that it includes an option to search the Internet, and another named Computers or People (Figure 7.3).

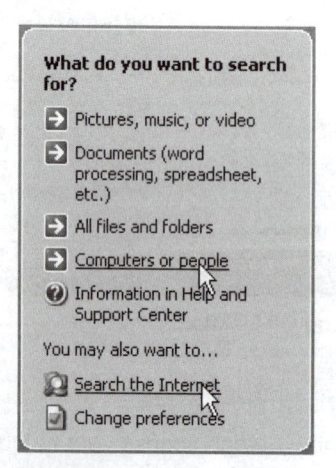

Figure 7.3 The search functions on the Internet.

Click on the Internet link and the search window opens. In the panel on the left, you may either choose a category from the list or type in a couple of keywords. Either way, click the **Find** button and a list of results will appear in the right-hand panel (Figure 7.4).

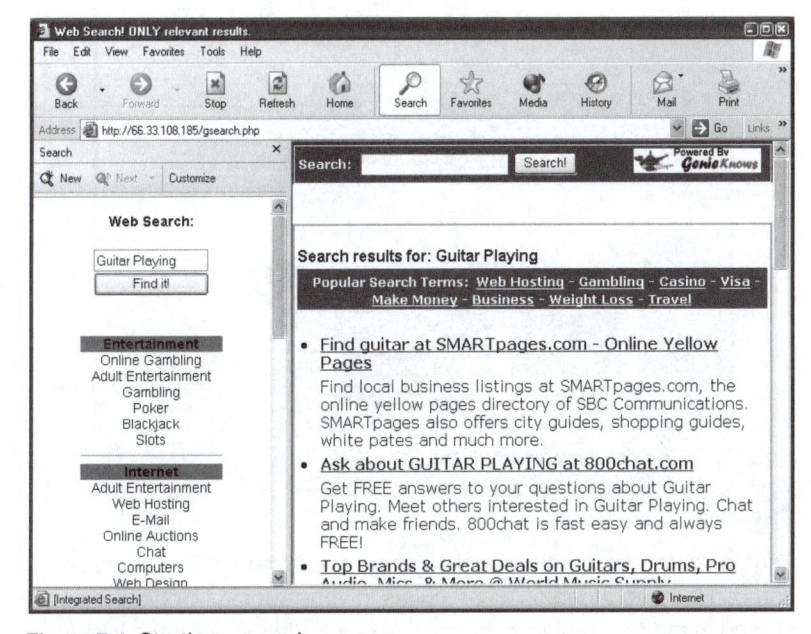

Figure 7.4 Starting a search.

You may then scroll down the list of results, which normally appear as a blue underlined heading followed by some descriptive text. The blue underlined text is a hyperlink, and clicking on it will open your browser (usually Internet Explorer or Netscape) with the selected page (Figure 7.5). Your results remain accessible in the search window so that you can browse through other search results.

Information

Improve your search skills The Web offers hundreds of search engines, directories, metasearchers and search tools. Each has its particular advantages and individual features. You would not, for example, use the same tool to look for a virtual travel agency, access a Web shop or call up a software product.

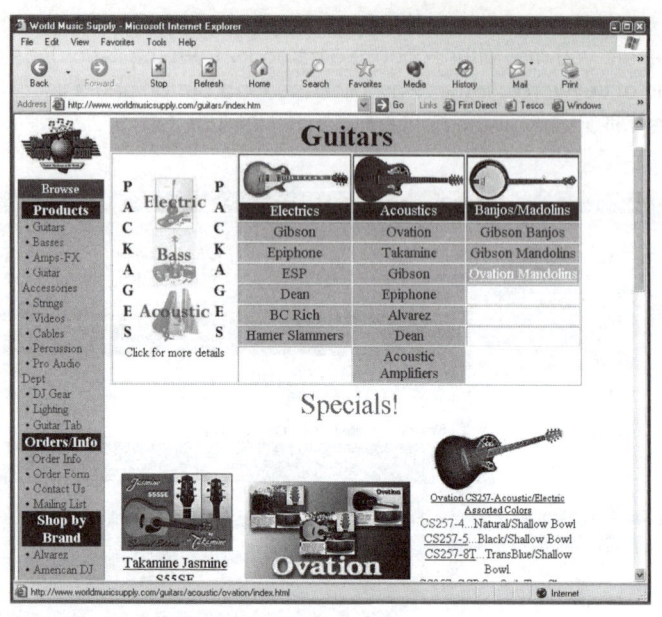

Figure 7.5 The first search result from the Web.

Paging

Paging (searching for individuals) can be conducted offline or online. You can look up a person's particulars in your Address Book (the one offered in the messaging software Outlook Express) or on the Web using the extensive search engines offered.

Searches in the Address Book are based on name, address, e-mail address or telephone number.

From the Search window, click on **Computers or People**. Then click **People** in your address book and enter the keywords in the spaces provided in the window (Figure 7.6).

There are paging directories and search engines on the Web, such as FourII, Bigfoot, InfoSpace, WhoWhere and Switchboard. If you are looking for the e-mail address of someone whose surname you know, these search engines can be really useful. Choose the option Search the Internet.

Executing a command

The Run option in the Start menu has a new feature in Windows XP. You can still fill in the name and path to a program you wish to run, but now you can enter a Web address (URL) directly (Figure 7.7).

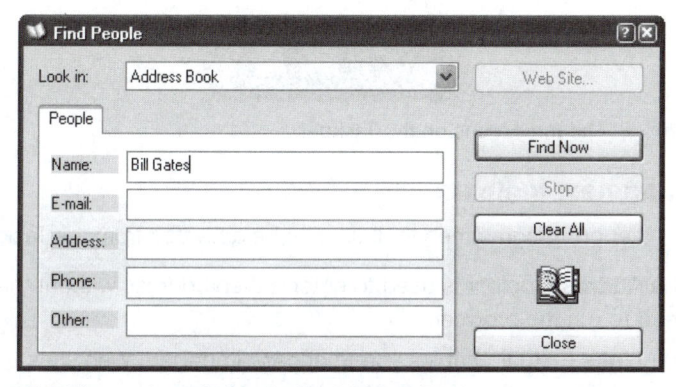

Figure 7.6 The paging window in the Address Book.

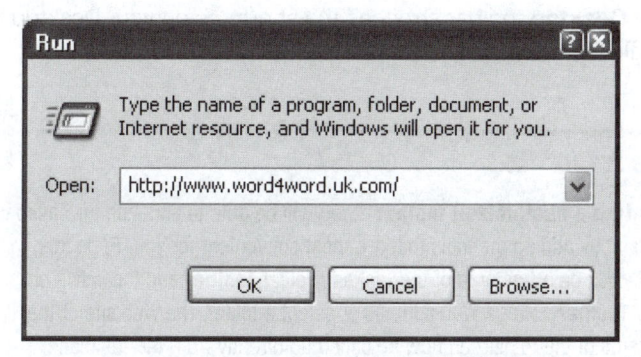

Figure 7.7 Entering a Web address and logging on directly.

→ The Taskbar

Just to the right of the Start button there will be several small icons.

The Quick Launch bar

These icons perform the following functions (from left to right in Figure 7.8):

- Start Internet Explorer 6.0.
- Start Outlook Express.
- Quick return to the Windows XP Desktop: one click on this icon minimizes the windows of active applications. Those applications can still be called up from the Taskbar. Just click on the icon again to go back to your original applications.

Windows XP and the Internet   **81**

Figure 7.8 The three icons on the Taskbar.

Adding new toolbars

Four other pre-programmed toolbars can be activated from the Taskbar:

- The **Address** toolbar is used to enter a Web address without the need to run the browser.
- The **Links** toolbar enables you to access important Web sites without the need to open the browser.
- The **Language** toolbar allows you to switch languages.
- The **Desktop** toolbar arranges the shortcuts on your Desktop in a single location.

> **Timesaver tip**
>
> **Creating a customized toolbar** You will be able to enhance the Taskbar yourself by adding the tools that are most convenient for you. To do this, right-click on a free area of the Taskbar, select **Toolbar** and then click on **New Toolbar**. Enter a Web address or select a folder. The Web site or the contents of the folder can now be called up directly from the Taskbar.

To display and use these toolbars:

1. Right-click on a free area of the Taskbar.
2. Select **Toolbars**.
3. Click on **Address**, **Links** or **Desktop**, as you wish (Figure 7.9).

> **Timesaver tip**
>
> **Adjusting a customized toolbar** The settings for this customized toolbar can be altered to suit your needs. You can easily adjust its size by increasing or decreasing its width. Move the cursor on the edge. When it changes to a two-headed arrow, drag it left or right as you wish. You can also move the bar away from the edge of the screen. To do this, click on the top part of the bar; when the cursor changes appearance, bring the toolbar to the middle of the screen. Position it and adjust its size as you wish.

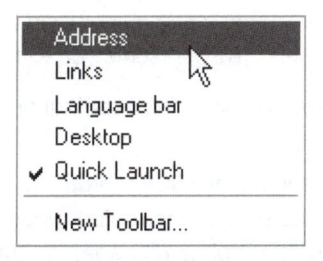

Figure 7.9 Adding a toolbar to the Taskbar.

Creating a toolbar on the Desktop

If the toolbar is overcrowded, you can create a toolbar on the Desktop from any folder. That folder may contain other folders, documents or Web addresses.

This procedure is straightforward. Click on a folder, then keeping the mouse button pressed, drag it to the edge of the screen, as in Figure 7.10. Release the mouse button and the folder contents can then be accessed directly from a vertical bar.

Figure 7.10 One toolbar has been moved from the edge of the screen and placed on the Windows XP Desktop. The other remains at the edge.

Windows XP and the Internet   **83**

By right-clicking on a free area of the customized toolbar, you can open the context-sensitive menu. This presents you with a number of settings:

- Display objects as large (the default setting) or reduced size (**View**, **Large** or **Small**).

- Hide the toolbar automatically (**Auto-hide**). When the cursor drops below the edge of the screen, the toolbar pops up; as soon as the cursor moves away, the toolbar disappears. Only a vertical line (or a horizontal line, if the toolbar is positioned at the top or bottom of the screen) is visible when the bar is not open.

> **Important**
>
> **Hiding a toolbar** You can only hide a toolbar positioned at the edge of the screen; this feature does not work if the toolbar is positioned in the middle of the Desktop.

→ Windows Explorer

We will now look at some of the features offered by Explorer. Due to the increasing popularity of the Internet, we now need to be able to work on objects stored on the hard disk and resident on Internet servers. Microsoft has thus adapted the Windows Explorer accordingly.

As the folders are scanned, you can call up the results pages using the Back and Forward buttons on the toolbar. With the Search, Favorites, History and Channels buttons, the Explorer acts like a browser.

To start Windows Explorer, click on **Start**, **All Programs**, **Accessories**, **Windows Explorer** (Figure 7.11).

The Windows Explorer components are as follows:

- **Toolbar**. The new buttons, Back and Forward, are used to scan pages. Use the Up folder to go back through the tree structure.

- **Address bar**. To input a path on the hard disk or even an Internet address.

- **Left-hand pane**. Shows the tree structure of the disk being explored. The + sign means a folder contains subfolders.

- **Right-hand pane**. Shows the results of the exploration.

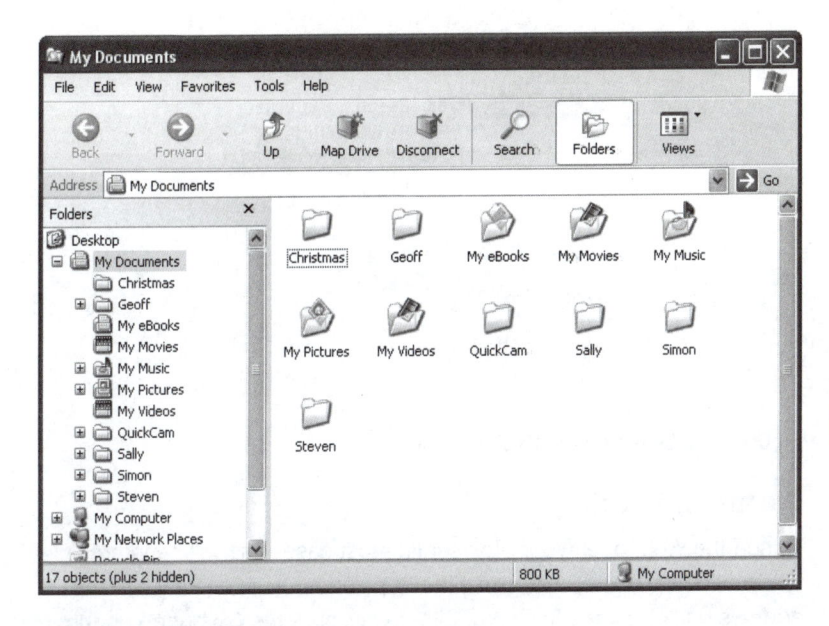

Figure 7.11 Windows Explorer.

Windows Explorer handles the folder contents display windows: as you browse, you can call up the results pages using the Back and Forward buttons. The toolbar also has a Properties button, which gives you immediate access to the Properties window for the object selected. Click on the **View** button to select the display mode (large icons, small icons, list and details). A Thumbnails option will also be offered for most folders.

The various browsing methods offered can be called up from the View menu (top left) by selecting **Explorer Bar** (Figure 7.12):

- **Search**. Activates a search engine on the Web.
- **Favorites**. Opens a list of folders containing your Internet favourites.
- **Media**. Open folders containing video clips, music, pictures, etc.
- **History**. Opens a history file of past searches.
- **Folders**. This is the conventional system-wide exploring mode.

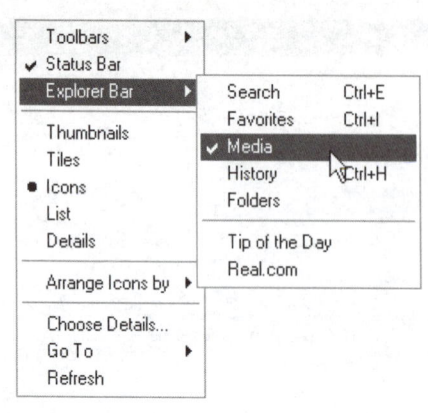

```
Toolbars          ▶
✓ Status Bar
  Explorer Bar    ▶    Search      Ctrl+E
                       Favorites   Ctrl+I
  Thumbnails         ✓ Media
  Tiles                History     Ctrl+H
● Icons                Folders
  List
  Details              Tip of the Day
                       Real.com
  Arrange Icons by  ▶

  Choose Details...
  Go To             ▶
  Refresh
```

Figure 7.12 Selecting the Explorer Bar.

Surfing the Web

To surf the Web, open your browser (in most cases this will be Internet Explorer or Netscape). You can either type an address directly into the address bar, or enter a keyword. Either way, click the **Go** button on the right. If you have entered a Web address, and the address exists and you have typed it correctly, the page will be displayed. If you have entered a keyword, a search will be made and several links will eventually be displayed. Click on a link and the page will then be displayed.

Most Web pages contain links, which when clicked upon will take you to another page.

> **Timesaver tip**
>
> **Displaying a Web site in optimum conditions** Once you have found the site you want, you will often find it easier to view the page in full-screen mode. Click on the **Full screen** icon on the Explorer toolbar. The Explorer pane vanishes and the page occupies the entire screen. You can even hide the small toolbar temporarily: right-click on a free area of the bar and select **Auto-hide**.

Adding a page to Favorites

You can easily add Web pages to your Favorites list. Right-click on the page, then select **Add To Favorites** from the menu that appears (Figure 7.13).

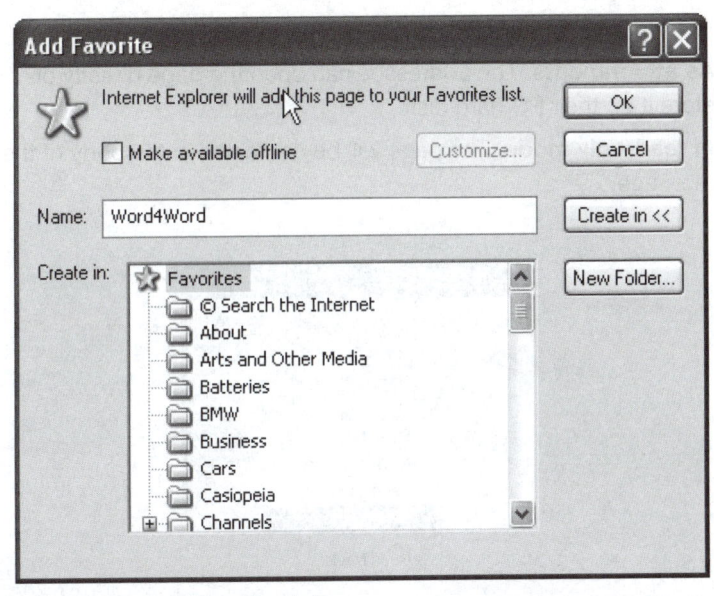

Figure 7.13 The Add Favorite dialog.

If you tick Make available offline, Explorer will download and store pages so that you can read them later. The Customize button runs a wizard where you can define which pages to download and when to do it. The Name may need editing to make it more meaningful. If desired, you can choose which Favorites folder to create the new link in.

> **Important**
>
> **Arranging your favourite sites** When you add sites to the Favorites menu, you can choose which folder to place it in, or let it be added to the main list. If need be you can rearrange your favourites: in Explorer, click on **Favorites**, **Organize Favorites**. Alternatively, click on **Favorites**, click on the Web site to be moved, then keeping the mouse button pressed, drag it to the chosen folder.

Sending a Web page by e-mail

The Internet Explorer toolbar contains a Mail icon (Figure 7.14), which allows you to send the site link (or the page itself) to another party. This is a very practical way of sharing your Internet discoveries with fellow Net users.

You can send pages:

- **As attachments**. The addressee can open the page directly or store it on their PC hard disk.
- **In read-only mode**. The page will be contained in the body of the message.

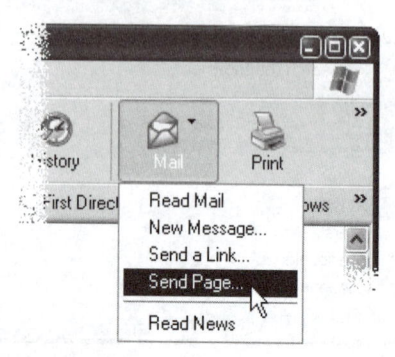

Figure 7.14 Sending a page by e-mail.

→ The Windows XP Desktop in Web style

With Windows XP, you will discover new ways of working with the Windows Desktop.

To switch to Web style:

1 Double-click the **My Computer** icon which is displayed on the Desktop.

2 Select **Tools**, **Folder Options** (Figure 7.15).

3 Choose the radio button labelled Single click to open. This will make the next two options available (previously they were greyed out and hence unselectable).

4 Select Underline icon titles consistent with my browser.

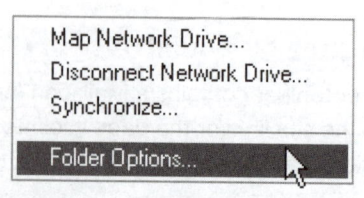

Figure 7.15 The Folder Options command.

> **Timesaver tip**
>
> **Classic operating style** If you want to go back to classic operating style, you can cancel Web style. To do this, bring up the Folder Options menu and select the **Classic style** options on the General tab.

→ Folder settings

There are other ways in which you can customize the folders. Still on the General tab of the Folder Options dialog, you may choose to open each folder in its own window rather than replacing the contents in the same window (Figure 7.16). You may also prefer to use the old-style folders by clicking Use Windows classic folders.

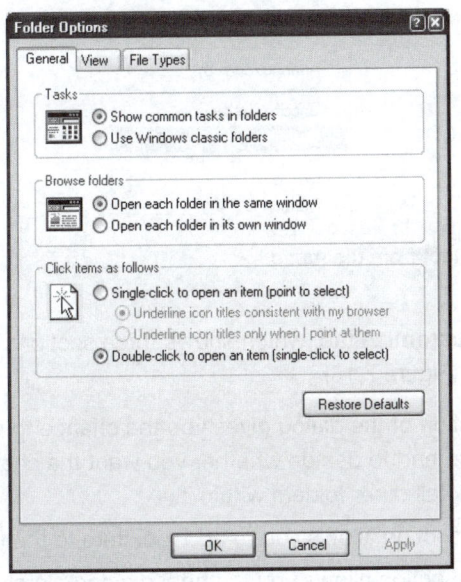

Figure 7.16 The General tab offers several customizing options.

Folder display settings

You will observe that the contents of folders are now displayed as links, similar to Web pages. Each constituent object (whether it is a file or a folder) is a link that you can open with a single click. You can do all sorts of things with these Web pages; the Folder Display Wizard in particular will help you in your task.

Windows XP and the Internet **89**

You may further customize folders as follows:

1 Select the folder by pointing the cursor at it. You will see that information about the folder appears on the left-hand side of the window in the Details panel (name, file size, date of last modification, etc.).

2 Click on **View**.

3 Select **Customize This Folder** (Figure 7.17).

4 A dialog opens that will be headed (name of folder) Properties.

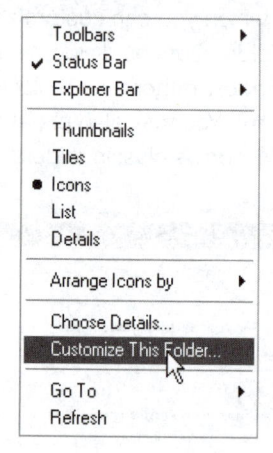

```
Toolbars              ▶
✓ Status Bar
  Explorer Bar        ▶

  Thumbnails
  Tiles
● Icons
  List
  Details

  Arrange Icons by    ▶

  Choose Details...
  Customize This Folder...

  Go To               ▶
  Refresh
```

Figure 7.17 Select from the menu.

Choose the **Customize** tab, which shows three sections for customization (Figure 7.18).

- The top section of the dialog gives you the chance to choose the type of folder and to decide whether you want the characteristics to be applied to all other folders within it.
- The middle section allows you to add a picture to the folder icon.
- The bottom section allows you to choose a completely different icon from the standard folder icon.

If you choose to add a picture to the folder icon, you can browse through other folders to find a suitable picture that would normally be in .BMP, .GIF or .JPG format.

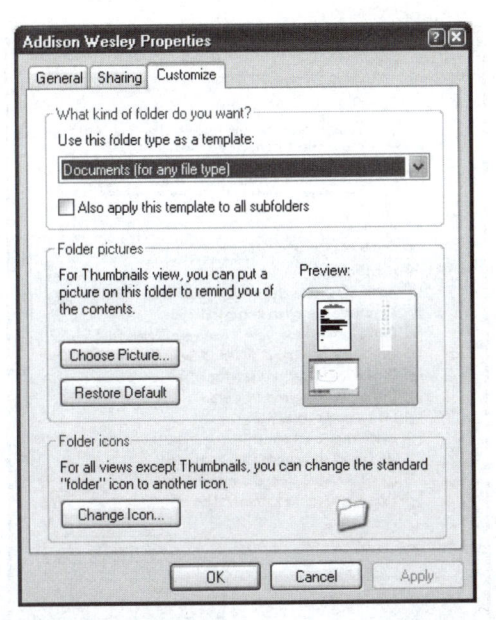

Figure 7.18 The folder properties.

Display settings for all files

We have just discussed folder presentation and customization methods. There is also a group of settings that governs the display and the way in which we work with all the files resident in the PC. From the Tools menu, select **Folder Options**, **View** (Figure 7.19).

Now choose the files and folders options that suit your needs; you can also decide to display the file attributes in detailed mode, display hidden files, or use layout settings such as font scaling. Use these options as you wish, but remember that the default settings are adequate most of the time.

Image file management

A major new feature in the image file management facility allows you to view the contents of an image file in thumbnail form before you open it in a software package. Use the **Thumbnails View** to see all the files in the folder in this way. Just click on the icon of the file to see file details in the left-hand panel (Figure 7.20).

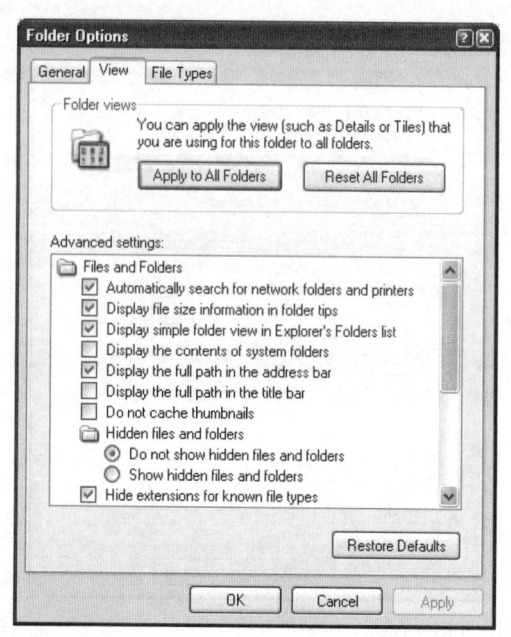

Figure 7.19 Folder display options.

Figure 7.20 Displaying the files as picture icons.

92 Brilliant Microsoft® Windows XP Pocket Book

The My Computer folder

To obtain details about hardware, go to the Desktop, click **My Computer** and select the disk drive [C:]. The total disk space and the space available are shown on the left-hand side of the display window (Figure 7.21).

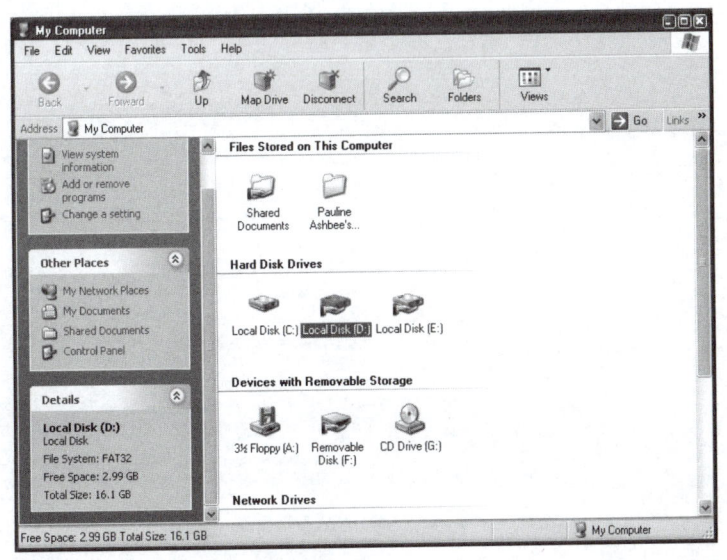

Figure 7.21 My Computer, by pointing to hard disk, you can obtain details of the total disk space and the free space.

8 Internet connection and Home Networking

To log on to the Internet, your PC must incorporate a program that can handle interchanges with the network. Do not forget that so-called 'personal' computers are designed to work independently and any connection to a network is based on the assumption that there is an interface. These add-ons may be supplied with the operating system, in which case you just need to install them.

When you access the Internet, the connection (log-on) program performs the following tasks:

- It sets up the link to the site of your Internet access provider (IAP).
- It handles the data interchange protocol used on the Internet.

→ The Internet connection

Your first attempt to access the Internet can be a tricky operation because you may be required to set up a string of parameters. However, the data to be entered are too technical for most users. Remember also that what works on another machine may not necessarily work on yours. Your Internet Service Provider should supply you with all the necessary information. Most also provide you with installation programs that handle the bulk of the work for you. Once you have set the Internet parameters, you do not have to reset them.

There are several ways to set up the log-on parameters:

- Use the automated installation script supplied by your access provider.
- Register a dial-up connection.
- Use the Windows XP Connection Wizard.

The first method automates your dial-up networking. The second can be tricky, but is worth knowing and is the one we will be looking at in detail.

→ Setting up a dial-up connection

From the Control Panel, click on **Network and Internet Connections**, then choose Create a connection to the Internet. This starts the Connection Wizard (Figure 8.1).

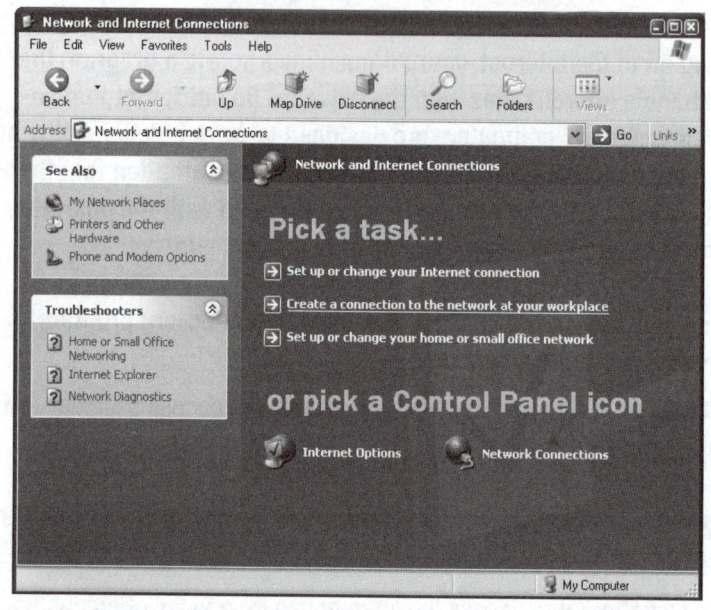

Figure 8.1 Choosing the Connection Wizard from Network and Internet Connections in the Control Panel.

If you want to establish a connection using a modem and your telephone line (the most common arrangement), select **Dial-up Connection** and click the **Next** button.

As you will see later, you can register several connections.

In the New Connection Wizard, choose a name for the connection (Figure 8.2), click **Next** and enter the dial-up number of your Internet Service Provider (Figure 8.3). Click **Next** after each 'page' and finally click the **Finish** button to end the wizard.

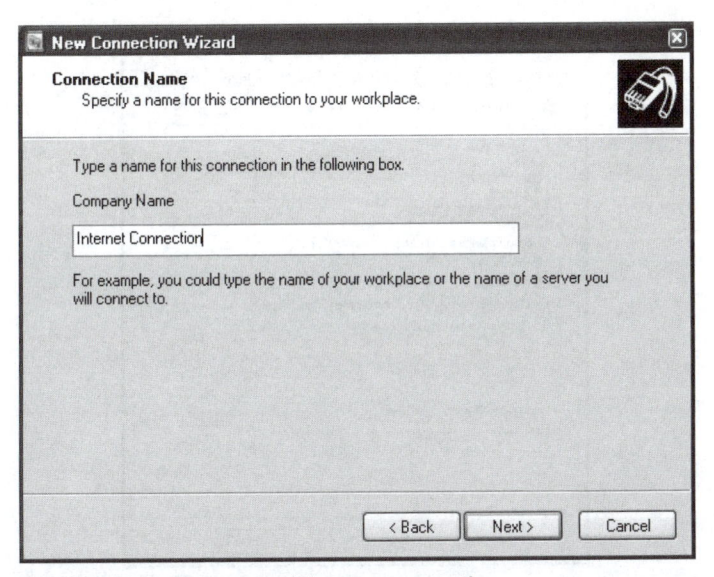

Figure 8.2 Entering the name of the new connection.

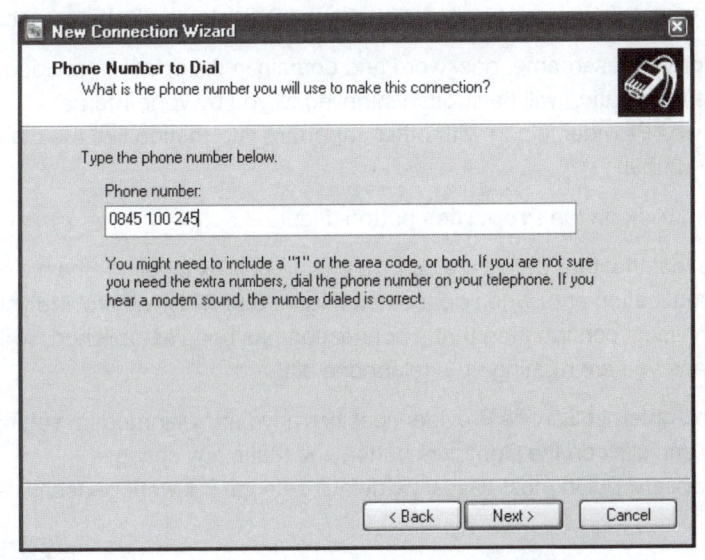

Figure 8.3 Entering the dial-up number of your service provider.

Now choose Internet Options from the Control Panel and click on the **Connections** tab. You should see the connection that you have just entered (Figure 8.4).

Internet connection and Home Networking   **97**

Figure 8.4 The Internet Properties dialog.

Click once on your new connection and then click on the **Settings** button.

Enter your username, password and domain in the spaces provided. This information will have been supplied to you by your Internet Service Provider, along with other important information like the dial-up number.

Next, click on the **Properties** button (Figure 8.5).

The main feature of this dialog is to check the box labelled Show icon in notification area when connected (Figure 8.6). This will provide you with visual confirmation that a connection has been established, which means you are running up a telephone bill.

If your Internet Service Provider specifies any particular modem settings, you can click on the Configure button and make any changes necessary, but in most cases the default settings will work perfectly well.

Important

Check your Internet access provider options Generally, the access provider procedure is designed for a specific browser. Get all the necessary details beforehand and make it clear that you will be using Windows XP and Internet Explorer 6.0.

98   Brilliant Microsoft® Windows XP Pocket Book

Figure 8.5 The Settings dialog.

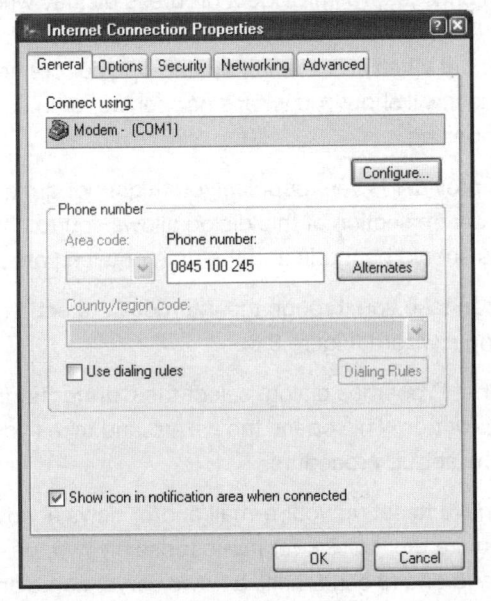

Figure 8.6 Internet Connection Properties dialog.

the Options tab, you have a few check boxes that are worth selecting (Figure 8.7).

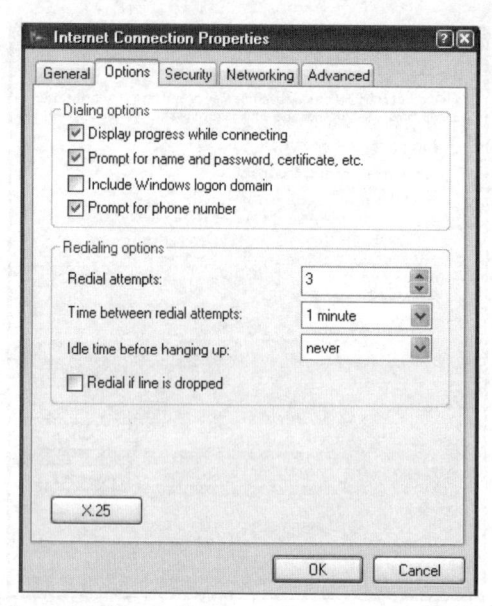

Figure 8.7 Further options may be found on the Options tab.

The top box, if checked, will provide a progress display while connecting to the Internet. This is a particularly annoying feature for long-term use, but when you are first setting up your connection it is worth having as it will show you what's happening, or in some cases, what's not happening.

If your service provider is very popular, you might not get a connection first time. The centre section of this dialog allows you to choose how many attempts should be made and the time between attempts.

Windows XP can take you through the Internet Connection set-up procedure using a wizard (Figure 8.8).

From the Internet Properties dialog, select the **Connections** tab and click the **Setup** button. This opens the wizard and takes you step by step through the set-up procedure.

You may also have to set up your e-mail and/or news account. To do this you will require the mail server name (possibly two: one for received mail and one to send mail), a news server name and your own e-mail address. Again, this information will be provided by your Internet Service Provider.

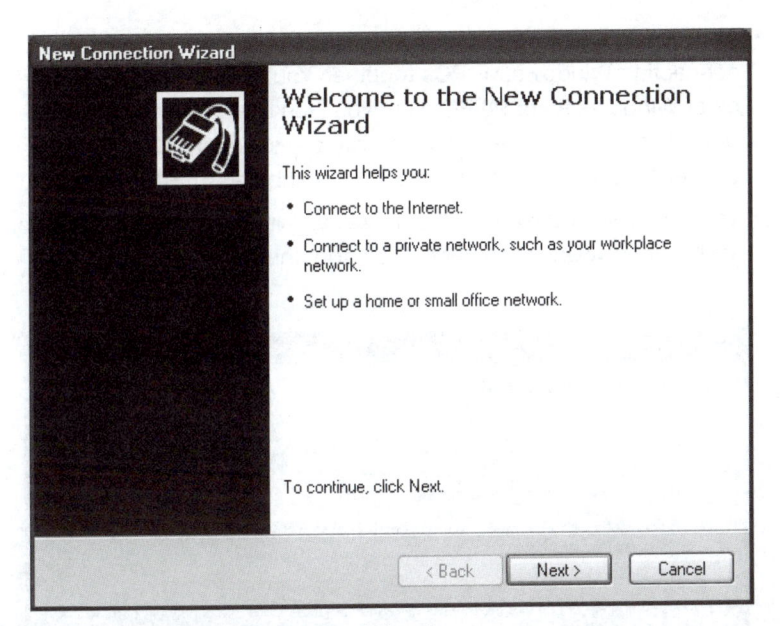

Figure 8.8 The Internet Connection Wizard.

→ Home Networking

Many people will skip over this section, feeling that it is not something they need concern themselves with. The fact is that building a network from two or more computers in your home can provide some very real benefits.

- More than one computer can share a single Internet connection. Each computer behaves as if it has its own 'private' connection.
- Files on one computer can be backed up on to another. This is particularly important if you carry a laptop computer to and from your workplace.
- Each computer is able to share common resources. Rather than having a printer each, you can have just one printer and allow everyone to share it. This applies equally to CD-ROM drives, scanners and many other peripherals.

Setting up even a small network used to be a real chore. Windows 95 introduced some tools which simplified it, but it was still not a job for the faint-hearted or the non-technical. But the Home Networking Wizard transforms the business. It is so easy to use – with two provisos.

- Networking is quite straightforward as long as you are just connecting Windows XP PCs together. You can also connect to older Windows 95 or 98 PCs, but you won't get quite the full range of facilities through the link. If you want to share an Internet connection, the PC with the modem must be an XP PC.

- You still have to open the PCs' boxes and install the network cards, and their software, then cable them together.

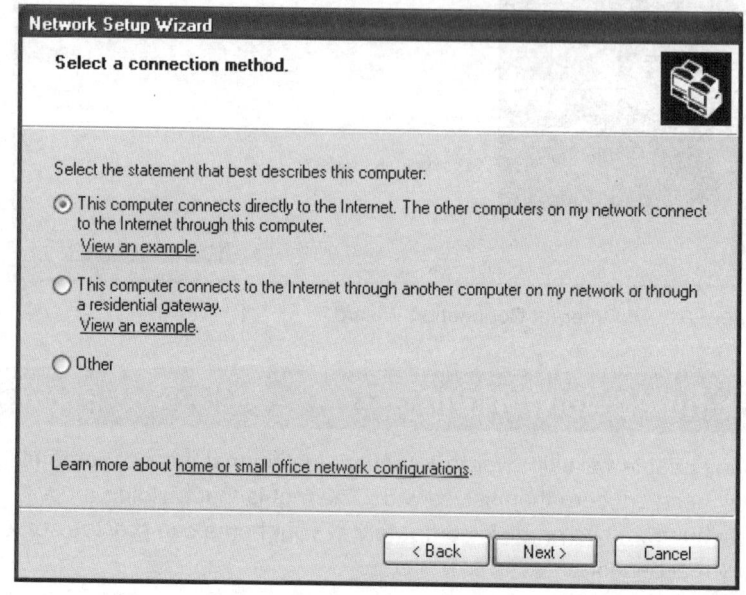

Figure 8.9 Starting to work through the Home Networking Wizard. If the PC has an Internet connection, the wizard will ask for details.

The Home Networking Wizard takes care of setting up the Windows networking software. All you need to do is tell the wizard a few things about your system (Figure 8.9) and then decide what to call your machines (Figure 8.10) and which folders and printers to share – and that is it!

Important

ISPs and connection sharing Internet connection sharing may not work with some ISPs. If you have problems, check that the ISP can handle it.

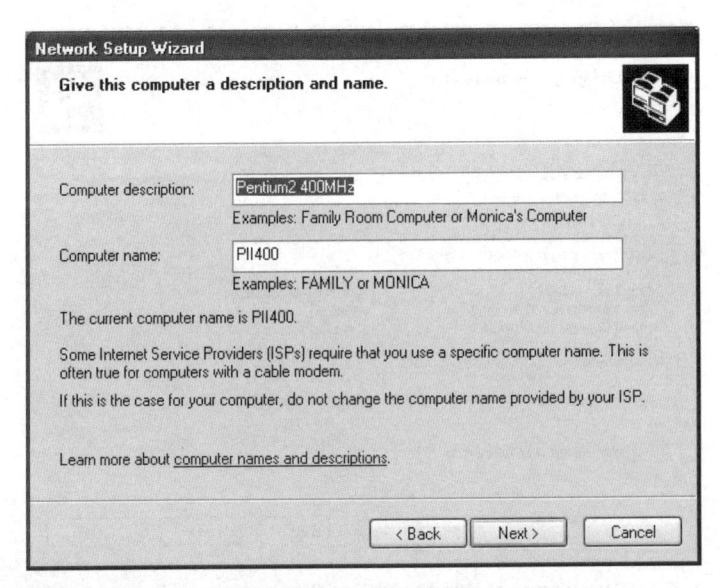

Figure 8.10 Each computer has to be given its own name.

Once the network is in place, you can then run the Internet Connection Wizard on the PC that does not have the modem. Tell it you want to set up the connection manually and through a LAN (Local Area Network).

This is the crucial stage. The PC with the Internet connection is acting as a 'proxy server' – one that makes the connection for another. Don't try to configure it yourself – that option is there for special situations and keen techies. Select Automatic discovery of proxy server and let the wizard sort it out for you (Figure 8.11). It may take a minute or so. The rest of the wizard collects details of your e-mail account.

The connection is fully shared. Not only can all the networked machines use the connection, they can use it at the same time.

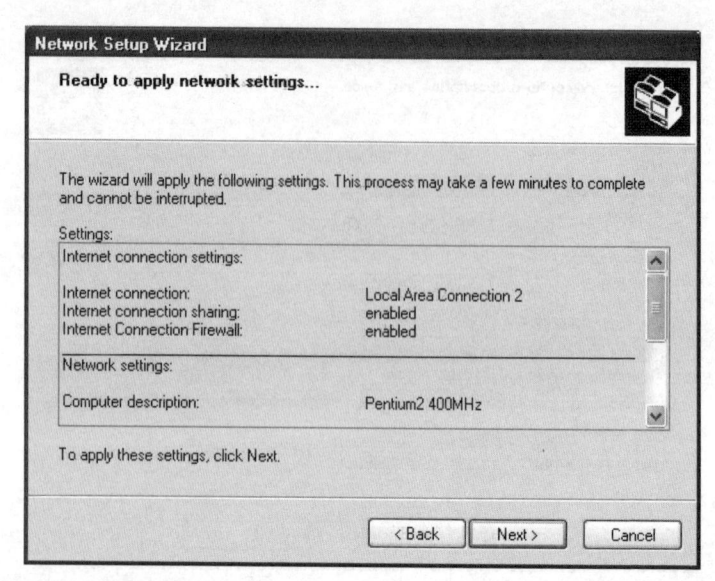

Figure 8.11 The beauty of Windows XP is that it works out all the settings for you.

9 The Internet Explorer browser

0Internet Explorer 6.0, a software package distributed free by Microsoft, is already installed with the Windows XP operating system.

In this version, Microsoft has made a number of small but significant improvements in the functionality and ease of use of its browser. The most visible changes are:

Search facility

The ability to sort the History list in different ways, making it simpler to revisit sites.

Organizing Favorites

The replacement of the 'channel' concept with a more useable method for storing pages and reading them offline.

An Autocomplete facility which offers to complete URLs for you when you start to type them into the Address bar.

Support for multiple connections

The MSN Messenger Service, which informs you when your friends are online.

Once your Internet connection has been set up you can surf the Web using all the resources your browser offers.

→ Running the browser

Internet Explorer 6.0 can be called up from **Start**, **All Programs**, **Internet Explorer**. You can also use the shortcut displayed on the Desktop or you can use the Quick Launch bar (to the right of the Start button) on the Taskbar.

When the browser opens, start the Internet log-on procedure by clicking **Connect**, if it is not set to do so automatically. The default home page will then be displayed (Figure 9.1).

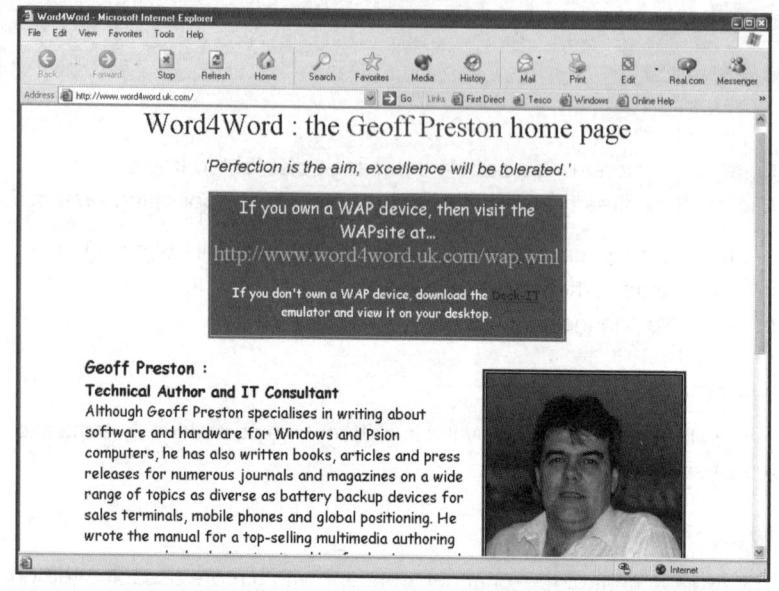

Figure 9.1 Opening the browser by displaying a default home page.

> **Timesaver tip**
>
> **Your home page** By default, the browser is configured to display a Microsoft site. To display a different site of your choice, click on **Tools**, **Internet Options**. In the General dialog, enter the URL (address) of your home page and confirm your choice by clicking **OK**. When you next run the browser, this is the page that will be displayed by default. A good idea is to use your favourite search engine as the home page. If you run a company, you could use your intranet welcome page as the default.

If you want to browse a Web page that you have stored locally or recorded using the History facility, you can work offline (saving on your telephone bill). The Work Offline box will be ticked in the File menu. If you try to open a page that you have not stored, a dialog will invite you to log on. To log on, either untick the Work Offline box, or click **Connect** in the dialog. This will open a dialog showing you that a connection is being made and giving you the chance to cancel (Figure 9.2).

Figure 9.2 Starting up an Internet connection.

If you click Cancel while the PC is connecting, the connection attempt is interrupted and the browser opens the Dial-up Connection window. You can alter the log-on settings (**Settings** button) if you wish, or choose to stay offline, or resume the connection procedure. If several users share the PC, it is at this point that you enter your log-on password (Figure 9.3).

Figure 9.3 Entering your password.

Register your password by ticking the Save password box – then you will not have to enter the password again.

The Internet Explorer browser **107**

> **Timesaver tip**
>
> **Are you ready to connect to the Internet?** If your Internet log-on settings have not yet been configured, call up Internet Options from the Tools menu. Click on the **Connections** tab, then click **Settings** (Figure 9.4). You can use this as a reference for your first Internet account (to call up an access provider), or to establish a new access account, or to gain access via a local area network (Figure 9.5). For further details, refer to Chapter 8.

Establishing or terminating your Internet connection

Most of the time, the log-on start-up routine is automated. Entering a Web address in the entry box or asking for a page update is sufficient for the browser to invite you to accept the connection.

Once you have established your connection, you can run your browser and surf the Web. A connection indicator is visible on the Taskbar (to the right).

To log off, right-click on the active connection icon and select **Disconnect**.

Click **Status** to check the speed of the log-on process, the quantity of data interchanged between the server and your PC, and the time elapsed (Figures 9.6 and 9.7).

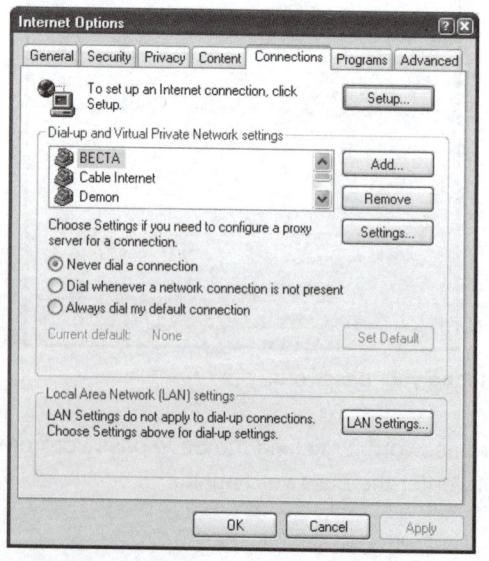

Figure 9.4 Internet log-on details

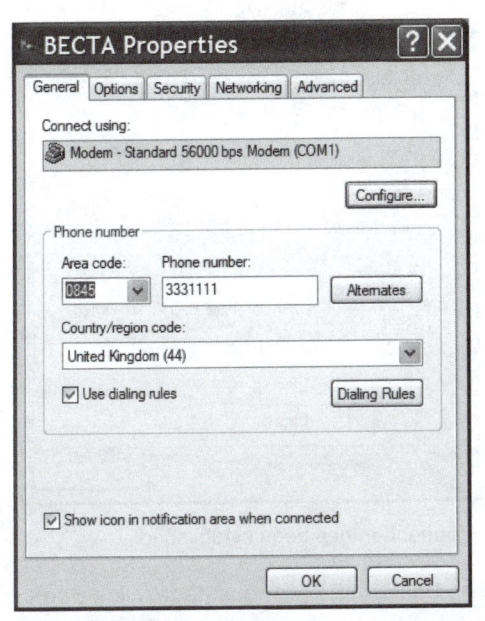

Figure 9.5 Starting the Internet connection routine without the browser.

Figure 9.6 Checking the status of the connection.

→ Browsing principles

Since everything begins with an address, enter one in the address bar (just under the toolbar). The address of your company, for instance, might be http://www.enterprise.com. If you enter the address incorrectly, you will be alerted. The error message 'nffl 404' means that the URL is not known.

The navigation buttons

If you have entered the address correctly, the page requested will then be displayed. You can then browse from that first page by clicking on the active links offered. The browser stores the pages displayed

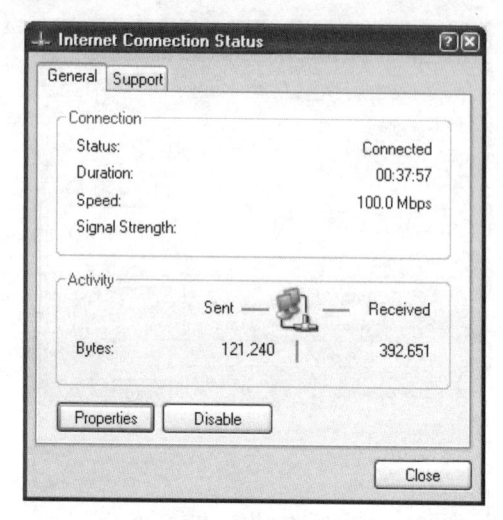

Figure 9.7 The connection has been established.

previously. To go back to the previous page, click **Back** on the toolbar. After you have gone back, you can display the following pages again by clicking **Forward**.

When loading a page, the browser icon, which is shown in reduced size at the top right of your browser screen, moves. At the same time, the information and the objects being loaded are shown on the status bar, at the bottom of the browser. When the page has been loaded, the icon stops moving.

You progress from one page to the next, from one site to another, or one service to another (and, sometimes, from one country to another) by clicking on the links offered. These links can assume all sorts of different shapes on a Web page. They are active areas and your browser shows them clearly by changing the appearance of the cursor: the arrow becomes a hand, meaning that you can access another page.

To return to a particular page, you can click several times on **Back** to return. Alternatively, click on the small down arrow to the right of the Back button to show a list of pages with their names (Figure 9.8). Click on the page you want to revisit. This is a practical way of quickly accessing a specific page.

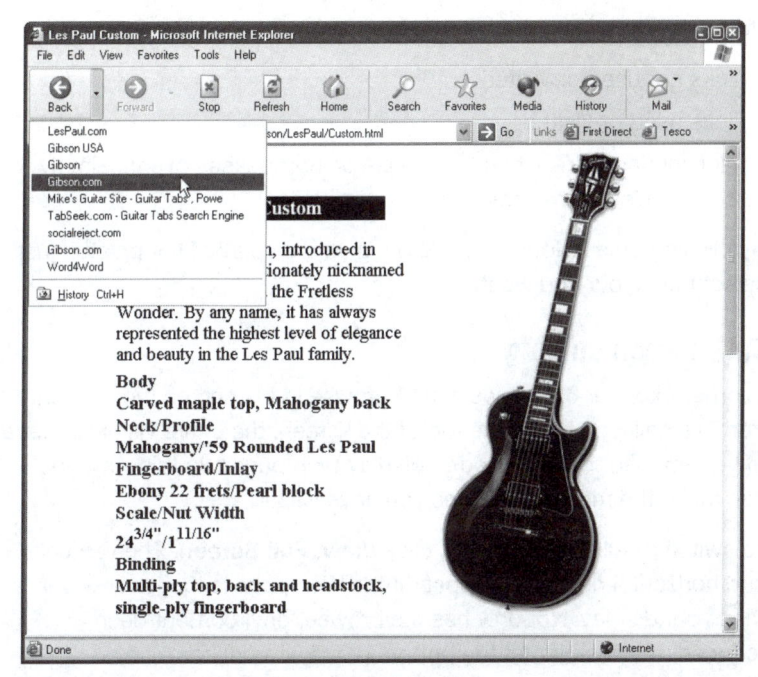

Figure 9.8 A list of pages displayed previously.

The History file

The History file stores details of your browsing over several log-on sessions. To display the History file, click on **History** on the toolbar. The History pane opens to the left of the browser. You can pick a specific date or display all the visits you have made earlier in the day.

If you click on a particular site, the pages of that site are then also listed. If you change sites, the previous list is closed and the list of pages at the new site is shown.

Displaying links

When a list is offered in the conventional way (in underlined text), you can check whether it has been used previously. This allows you, on a page with a number of links, to determine which links you might want to explore. The link colour changes the moment you use it. The colours of links that have and have not been activated can be programmed. Just go to the Internet Options feature in the Tools menu, click on the **General** tab, then select **Colors** at the bottom of the box.

The Internet Explorer browser   **111**

Here, you can define the colours for:

- links not used or visited
- links used or visited
- highlighting a link when the mouse pointer passes over it: simply tick the **Use hover color** box.

By clicking on a colour box, you bring up a display of the palette: just select the colour you want.

Full-screen surfing

Internet Explorer 6.0 allows you to browse in full-screen mode. Apart from a small icon bar at the top of the screen, the entire visible surface of your monitor can be used to display Web pages. In this way, you can make the most of the sites you have visited.

To switch to full-screen mode, click **View**, **Full Screen**. The vertical and horizontal risers only appear if the Web page is longer or wider than your display. Not only has the browser environment been reduced, the Taskbar (at the bottom of the screen) has also disappeared from the screen at the same time.

To return to classic style, press **F11** or click on the **Restore** icon at the top right of the screen.

In full-screen mode, you can go back to the previous page or display the next by opening the context-sensitive menu: right-click on a non-active area of the current Web page, then click **Back** or **Forward**.

> **Timesaver tip**
>
> **Total full screen**   To obtain a total full screen, you need to hide the reduced size full-screen bar. To do this, right-click a free area on the toolbar and select **Auto-hide**. The bar then disappears: it will not be displayed again until you point the cursor to the top of the screen. To get the bar back, point the cursor at the top of the screen, right-click in the bar, then untick **Auto-hide**.

Opening Web pages in a new window

It is possible to alter the way in which the results of all your Web requests are opened in the browser window, and to switch from one page to the next by pressing the **Forward** and **Back** buttons. This enables you to open pages in a new browser window. From the **File** menu, select **New**, **Window**: a new browser window opens. You can then switch between browsing operations in several windows without mixing up the Web pages you have received by using the tabs in the Taskbar.

Another option is to open a link, chosen from a Web page, in a new window. To do this, right-click on the link, and select **Open Link in New Window** (Figure 9.9).

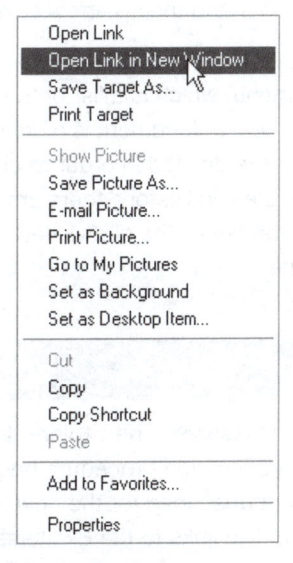

```
Open Link
Open Link in New Window
Save Target As...
Print Target

Show Picture
Save Picture As...
E-mail Picture...
Print Picture...
Go to My Pictures
Set as Background
Set as Desktop Item...

Cut
Copy
Copy Shortcut
Paste

Add to Favorites...

Properties
```

Figure 9.9 Opening a link in a new window.

Information

All sorts of links Usually, a link is shown as underlined text. But Web programming also allows a link to be assigned to an action button, a graphic or a map. A graphic can even comprise several links, depending on the place in which you click the mouse button. A drop-down list might also offer a series of access links. On certain Web pages, you can find specific icons representing the next or previous pages, inviting the user to browse a series of screens.

The Explorer Bar

The Explorer Bar opens to the left of the browser and allows you to view Web pages on the right-hand side of the screen, while you carry out searches and select options in the left-hand list. Of the lists offered, you will find History, Favorites, Channels and search results. You can access all these lists by clicking on the relevant buttons on the toolbar.

You can close the Explorer Bar by clicking on the cross at the top right of the frame. If the list is long, you can use the down arrow to display the rest of the links on offer and the up arrow to go back up the list.

A list contains objects, i.e. folders and addresses. When you click on a folder, you open a submenu, which is a list of the addresses entered in the folder. In your Favorites, a document is a subject (Hobbies, Finance, etc.) that you have defined in order to classify your Web sites to suit your particular tastes. In History, there are three organizational levels: the enquiry day (or week), the site visited, and the pages you looked up at a given site.

→ Web surfing

To start a search, click on **Search**. The explorer bar opens and, if you are offline, the Internet connection procedure begins. The operating mode is the same as that described for the new features of Windows Explorer. The search module links to the Excite search engine.

The Back and Forward buttons do not operate in the explorer pane, only in the main part of the browser. To conduct a new search, type the new keyword(s) in the search area and click **Search**. If the search does not find what you want, try going to a search engine site and search there. Three of the best are:

- Google at http://www.google.com, which has indexed over 1 billion pages.
- Jeeves at http://www.askjeeves.com, a very friendly place to start.
- Yahoo! at http://www.yahoo.com, which has millions of selected links to pages.

→ Managing your favourite Web sites

You should make your favourite site your home site. You have seen how it is possible to enter Web areas on the Desktop, and you can even choose an HTML page that would point to one of your favourite sites. To keep a record of your other favourite pages, store them in your Favorites folder. Favorites is a collection of folders and links that you can activate at any time.

Storing Favorites

To record a Web site in your Favorites list, select the Favorites menu and click **Add to Favorites**. You are now presented with a number of options (Figure 9.10):

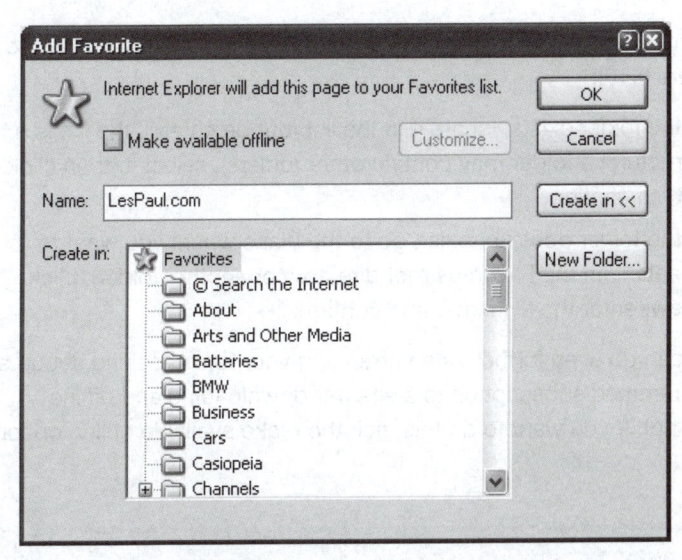

Figure 9.10 Storing a Web page in a Favorites folder.

- storing the page directly (or the link to the page) in the Favorites root directory
- storing the page in an existing folder
- creating a new folder for a new Web page subject.

A new name to the Web page you want to record in your Favorites will appear automatically. If the title is not self-explanatory, or if it is in another language, you can change its title. Click **OK** and the page will be stored in the root directory. In the list of Favorites, it will be visible at the end of the list after any folders. A good method is to store the pages systematically in folders and to define in advance (or when needed) the folder types.

> **Important**
>
> **Using the Favorites search tools** You can continue searching using the tools selected on the Web. Beforehand, you should have specified the search engines that you find the most useful in a Favorites folder. If you have done this, click on **Favorites**, select the relevant folder and click on one of the search engines. In this case, the search results will be displayed not in the explorer bar but on the overall page sent back by the search engine server.

To store a page in a folder, click **Create**. Two options are presented (Figure 9.10):

- If the folder exists, locate it in the list (but be careful, the list is a tree structure; a folder may contain other folders), select it, then click **OK** to confirm.
- If the folder does not exist, go to the place where you want to create it (in the Favorites root directory or another folder), click **New**, enter the filename, and confirm.

You can go even further when arranging your Favorites and set up a programmed subscription to a site (for downloading and offline reading). If you want to do this, tick the Make available offline option.

> **Timesaver tip**
>
> **Rearranging your Favorites** As time goes by, you might need to tidy your Favorites or rearrange them. You can delete a site, a complete folder or even transfer one folder to another. To do this, select the Favorites menu and click **Organize Favorites**. Click the folder you want to organize: you can now delete it, rename it, open it to fetch specific links, or move it to another location.

Scheduled downloading from a Web site

If you decide to subscribe to a site, simply check the Make available offline box. Then click **Customize** to set your subscription parameters. The Subscriptions Wizard will then do the rest (Figure 9.11).

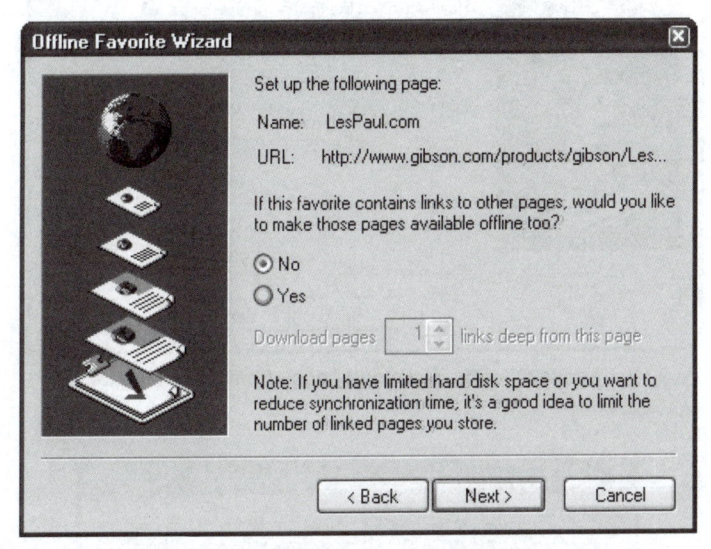

Figure 9.11 The wizard for subscribing to a Web site.

You can opt to download a Web page or part of the site (the page itself and any linked pages). To do this, tick one of the two options offered. Click **Next** to confirm.

You can now select when and how to synchronize with the site (i.e. download the latest pages). Your choices are:

- Download at any time that suits you by selecting **Synchronize** from the Tools menu.
- Create a new schedule (Figure 9.12).

If you choose to create a schedule, you will be asked to set the frequency and the time of day, and give a name for the schedule. If you find that you need to change the time later, you can redefine the schedule through the favourite's properties in the Synchronize dialog (Figure 9.13).

If you choose to use an existing schedule, you should then select one from the drop-down list.

At the next stage, you will be asked whether the site requires a username and password. If it does, they should be entered into the dialog.

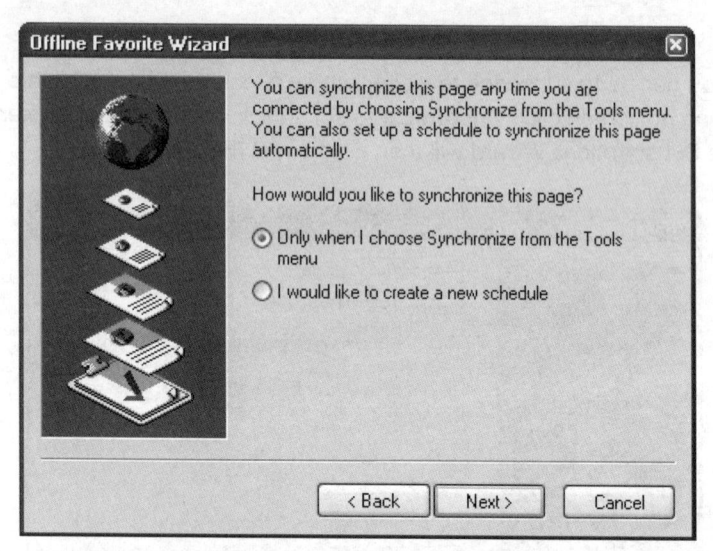

Figure 9.12 Choose when to download pages from the Web site.

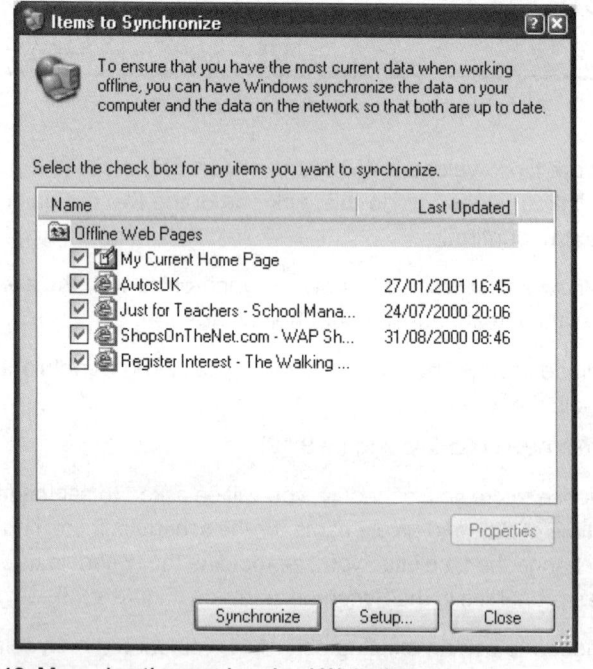

Figure 9.13 Managing the synchronized Web sites.

Once that is done, click **Finish** to end the wizard and return to the Add Favorites dialog. Click **OK** to save the settings and close the box.

You can handle all your offline sites through the Synchronize dialog. To open this, select the **Tools** menu and click **Synchronize**.

At the Synchronize dialog, you can synchronize selected sites, or edit their properties. If you need to change their schedules, you can access the schedule for a selected site through the Properties button, or access all the schedules through the Setup dialog.

→ Internet radio

With Internet Explorer you can now listen to radio broadcasts from all over the world through your PC. The radio reception is good, but not perfect. The problem is not in the quality of the sound, which is almost as good as a CD, but in its continuity. Modern compression techniques have greatly reduced the size of sound files, but they still take a lot of bandwidth, and there's not much to spare. If you get online through an ISDN line, you should have few problems. If you link through a dial-up connection, you will find that data comes in from the Web at rarely more than 2 Kb per second. That should be enough to cope with a broadcast, but if you are also surfing elsewhere, that will add to the overall quantity of data trying to come in. Expect occasional breaks in transmission of a second or so, and expect other sites to download slower.

If you want to listen to the radio, you must first turn on the Radio toolbar, from the View, Toolbars menu. Click on **Radio Stations** and select **Radio Station Guide**. This will take you to WindowsMedia (Figure 9.14), where you will find links to radio stations all over the world. There are hundreds of radio stations – far too many to show as a single list. Select a format, language, call sign or other feature to get a list of matching stations, then select from that. The station will be added to your own Radio Stations list, and can be selected from there next time you want to listen to it.

You do not have to be at the station's site to listen to a broadcast. You can start it playing, then surf on elsewhere.

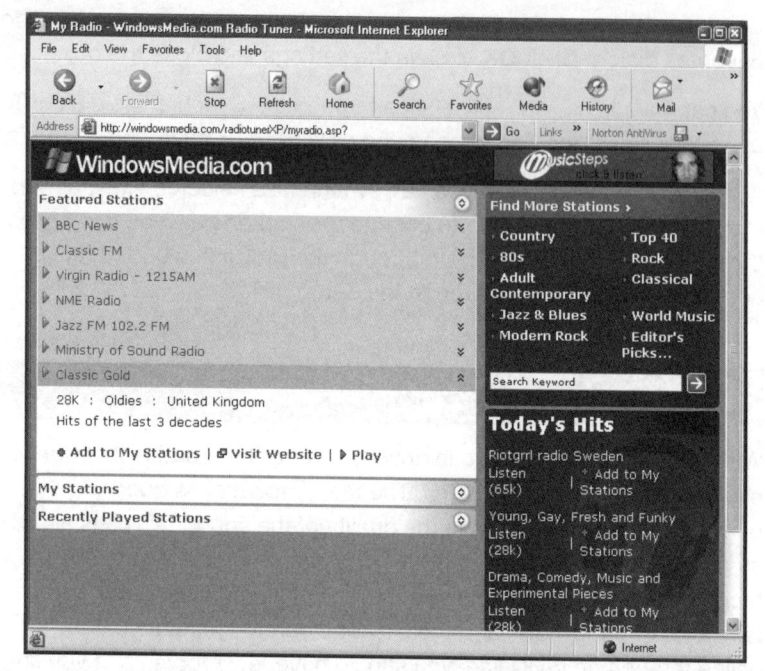

Figure 9.14 A great way to listen to radio from around the country, or from around the world.

Due to the number of connections an Internet radio broadcast may go through, there is a slight delay between the Internet station and a true live version. This can be as much as a couple of minutes, so don't set your clocks by it.

10 Electronic mail

Windows XP is supplied and installed complete with an electronic mail software package known as Outlook Express. Electronic mail, or e-mail as it is more widely known, is the most frequently used Internet tool.

Whether you use this facility in a private or business capacity, e-mail has become an indispensable tool.

Users of older versions of Internet Explorer may already have tried out Outlook Express. The software operates as a communications centre, managing, sending and receiving e-mail and messages from discussion groups. It incorporates an address book, and offers a wide range of features. Outlook Express replaced the communications centre offered in Windows 95, which was known as Microsoft Exchange. It is a program for sending messages and joining discussion groups using Internet standards. It represents a merger between Internet Mail and Internet News, which is a considerable step forward. Outlook Express allows you to configure your connection settings and manage mail efficiently, also enabling you to handle several Internet accounts. This is of value when you link a business account and a personal account; it is also practical in terms of sharing software at home.

As with any browser, the mail software can be called up from the Start menu, on the Desktop, or from the Quick Launch bar on the Taskbar.

The main software screen (Figure 10.1) shows the following components:

- the toolbar
- the mail document folders in the left-hand column (the display pane)
- access to major software features in the main frame.

When using the software for the first time, five default folders are available:

- **Inbox**. This contains the mail messages sent to you.
- **Outbox**. This contains all the mail written offline or to be sent later.

- **Sent Items folder.** This keeps a record of messages sent.
- **Deleted Items folder.** When a file is deleted, it is sent temporarily to this folder, unless you have configured the software settings differently. Remember to clear out messages in this folder regularly or request that the data be deleted when you quit the software.
- **Drafts folder.** This is a holding folder in which mail you are currently working on can be kept temporarily.

There may be an additional folder for the discussion forums suggested by the Internet access provider.

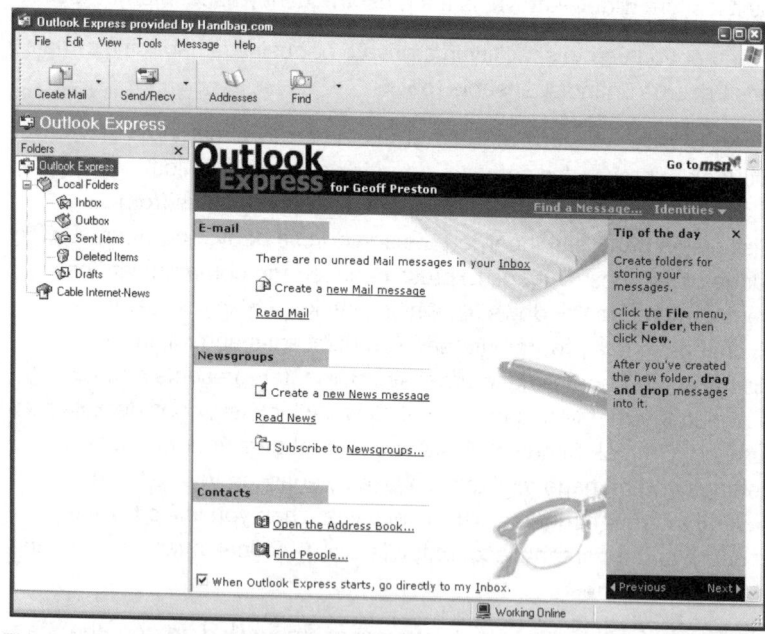

Figure 10.1 Outlook Express mail software

→ Handling your messages effectively

The Inbox may be less practical when you are dealing with a large number of messages. If you communicate with a large number of people, or if your e-mail address is published on Web sites or other media, or if you subscribe to information services supplied by e-mail, you will soon find out just how restrictive your single mailbox is. You therefore need to create new folders to store messages received (or, at least, those you wish to keep).

Creating document folders

Outlook Express enables you to handle a folder tree structure easily and to despatch your messages by subject. In this way, you can create an initial personal folder and another for business if you have a multipurpose account.

To create a new document folder, right-click on the Outlook Express root directory on the software explorer bar. From the context-sensitive menu select the **New Folder** command. Give the folder a name and then place it among the tree structure of existing folders. By doing this, you can create a new folder in an existing folder (Figure 10.2).

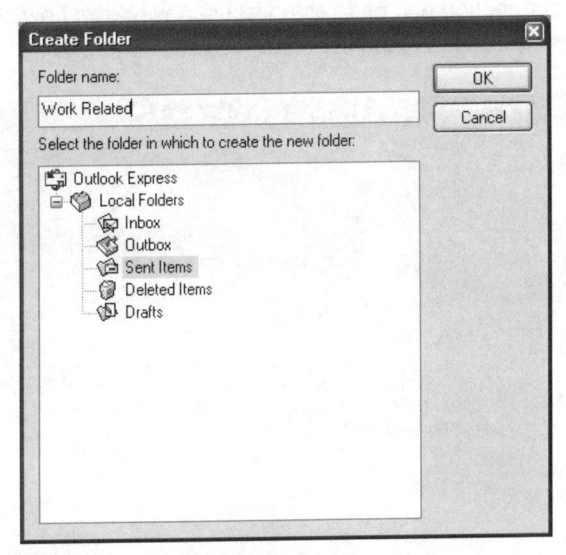

Figure 10.2 Creating a document folder.

Handling the arrival of new messages

By this stage, your Internet connection settings have been configured and your access provider server should be correctly identified. When starting up Outlook Express, the connection may be set up automatically, or you can log on at your request. You can also specify a start-up without logging on. This allows you, for example, to prepare mail offline, place it in the Outbox, and initiate a bulk despatch once you are online. In this way, you save on the cost of your calls. But you might also decide to start up the Internet connection every time you open the program in order to retrieve any new messages. To do this, go to the **Tools** menu and click **Options**. Select the **Connection** tab and tick the chosen option.

Electronic mail 123

You can configure other settings from the General tab in the Options window. For instance, you can check the arrival of new messages every hour. Irrespective of the automatic procedures you may have instituted to read your e-mail, you can also open your e-mail box at any time by clicking on **Send and Receive** on the Outlook Express toolbar.

When you click Send and Receive, the Send function is initiated first. All the messages that may be stored in the Outbox are then sent, so make sure you have drafted them properly (the right spelling, attachments present, etc.). If some messages are incomplete, you should store them in the Drafts folder before moving them to the Outbox.

Once the connection has been established, a window shows the progress of messages being sent and received (Figure 10.3).

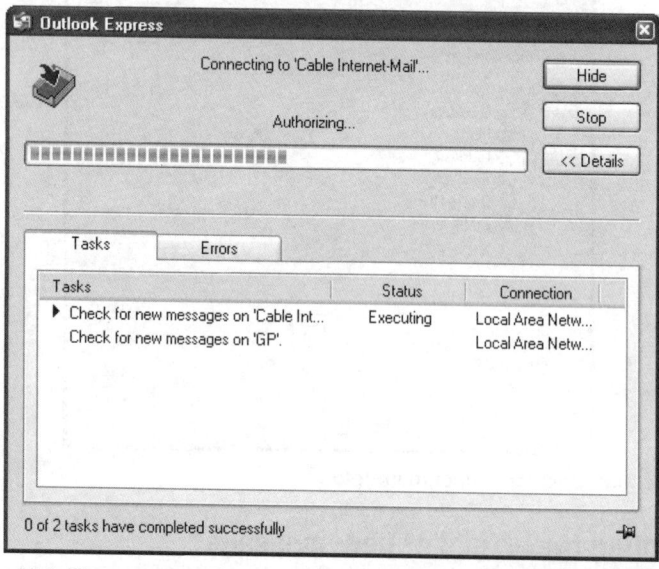

Figure 10.3 The progress of message transfer (messages sent and received).

The Details button in Figure 10.3 provides information on the tasks performed and any problems arising. If you tick the Hang up when finished button in the Details dialog, your line will be disconnected automatically when the sending tasks have finished and you have received any messages waiting.

> **Information**
>
> **Check your connection** From the Tools menu, click **Accounts**, **Mail**. Your access provider's mail server references are shown here. The Properties button enables you to fine-tune your settings (Figure 10.4).

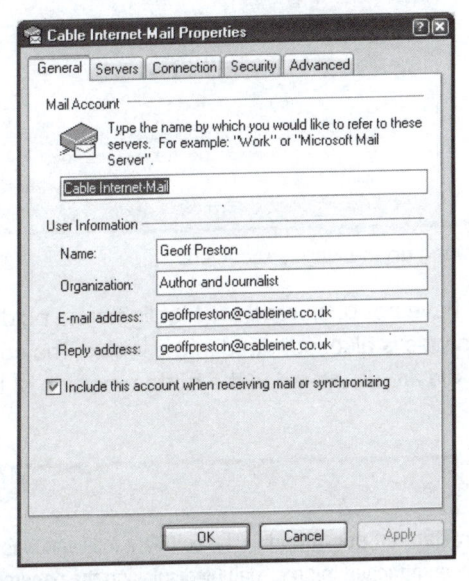

Figure 10.4 Mail account properties.

Looking up your messages

To check the messages you have received, click on **Inbox**. A list of the messages received is shown in the right-hand frame; at the bottom of the window, you will see the contents of the message selected in the list (Figure 10.5).

The Inbox has five components:

- the degree of urgency of the message (a red exclamation mark (!) means an important message is waiting)
- attached items (if the 'paperclip' icon is showing in this column)
- the name of the sender
- the subject of the message
- the date and time of receipt.

Electronic mail

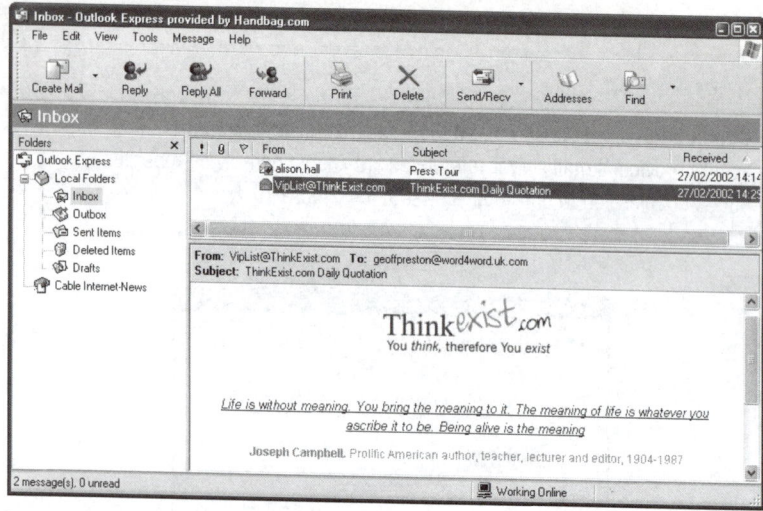

Figure 10.5 Looking up messages received.

Messages that have not been read are highlighted in bold. The number of unread messages is also indicated in the Inbox. The contents of the selected message are displayed in the bottom portion of the screen.

> **Information**
>
> **Displaying an attached document** The software tells you when a document has been attached to an e-mail by displaying the paperclip icon. Click on the message in question and then, in the reading area, click on the paperclip. The list of attachments is displayed. Click one of them and, depending on the document format, the appropriate software will start to run. Alternatively, click on the paperclip, then click **Save Attachments**. Choose where you want to save the attachment, then click **Save**.

Transferring a message

You can transfer a message from the Inbox to a storage file using the drag-and-drop facility. Similarly, you can right-click on the message and ask to move it. The same menu also allows you to send the message in question to someone else. To send a message you have received to another person, click **Forward** on the toolbar. A Send window opens, and you then specify the addressee.

Deleting a message

To delete a message, right-click, then click **Delete**, or click **Delete** on the toolbar. Items deleted are sent to the Deleted Items folder. To delete items permanently, click on the Deleted Items folder, then click **Edit**, **Empty 'Deleted items' Folder**.

Sorting messages

You may find it useful to sort the messages in your folders. By default, messages are stacked in date order: the one with the most recent date is at the top of the stack. To sort the messages, click the bar in the From/Subject/Received field. When you click **From**, you sort the messages by name in ascending order. When you click a second time, you reverse the order of the sort to descending order. You can revert to the initial dated sort by clicking **Received**.

You can also sort messages and put them into 'urgent' (red!) groupings, or group those with attachments (these are the first two fields on the field bar above the list). The sort functions can be called up from **View**, **Sort By**.

Drafting a message

To compose a message, click **Create Mail** on the Outlook Express toolbar. Complete the To, Cc and Subject fields, then type the message (Figure 10.6).

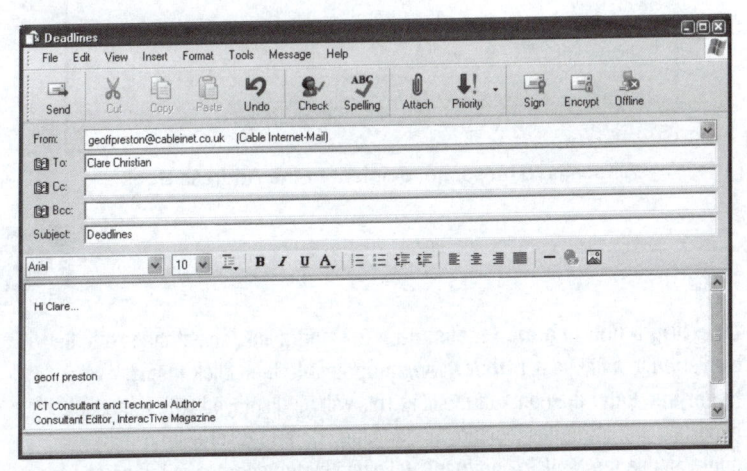

Figure 10.6 The message drafting window.

To enter the addressee's details, type the first few letters of his or her name. If there is a reference to the addressee in the Address Book, the Input Wizard suggests a complete name. Alternatively, click the book icon to the left of the input line to open the Address Book, and select your addressee (Figure 10.7). In the same way, you can specify those whom you wish to receive a copy (Cc; carbon copy). Their names will be seen by the other addressees. To hide the recipients of copies, use the line Bcc (blind carbon copy).

Once you have composed your message, click **Send**. Or, click **File**, **Send Later**. A message to be sent later is kept on hold in the Outbox. It will be sent, along with any others, the next time you activate **Send and Receive** on the software toolbar.

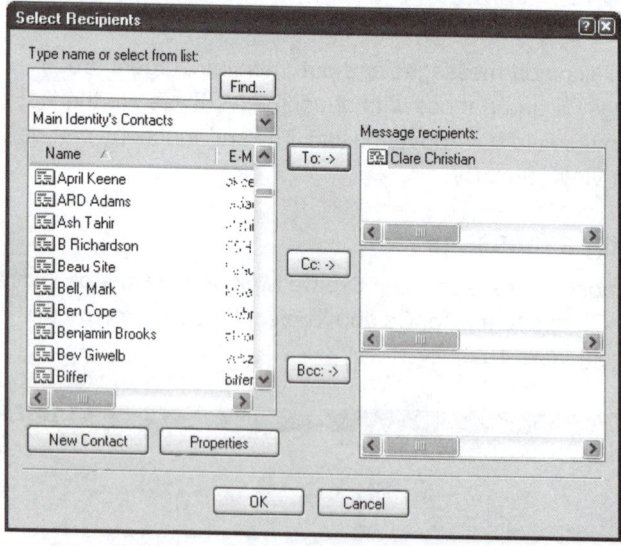

Figure 10.7 Choosing a message recipient in the Address Book.

Timesaver tip

Inserting a link in a mail message   To insert a link, select the text to be converted to a link, e.g. **http://www.company.uk**, then click **Insert**, **Hyperlink**. Enter the name of the link. This will be displayed with the usual hypertext link attributes (colours, underlining, etc.). To display an e-mail address, use the **Mail To** command, followed by the address of the person to contact. Your addressee can then click on the link to contact that address.

Timesaver tip

Using existing text You can prepare a message using the Windows Notepad or your usual word processor. Select the text, copy it (**Ctrl + C**) and, when you get back to the message drafting window, paste it in (**Ctrl + V**).

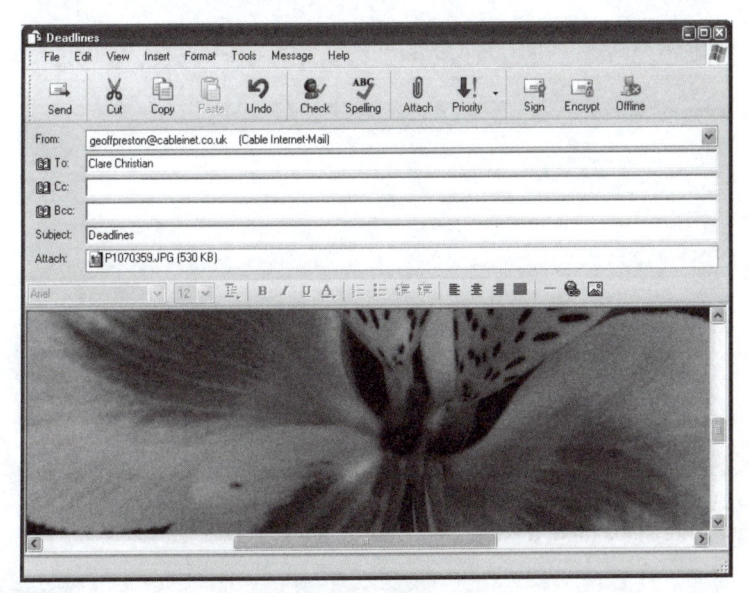

Figure 10.8 A message containing a picture.

Timesaver tip

Inserting a picture in a mail message To insert a picture, click the icon at the far right of the message drafting toolbar. In the window that then opens, enter the path to the picture file or browse the hard disk to locate it, then confirm. The picture appears in the message drafting window. You can select it, move it and resize it as you wish (Figure 10.8).

Inserting an attachment

One of the best features of e-mail is the ability to insert an attached document. You can append as many files as you wish and of any type to your outgoing mail.

To insert a file, click **Insert File Attachment**, then browse the hard disk to find the file you want. Repeat the operation as many times as you need.

The attached files are summarized at the bottom of the message drafting window (Figure 10.9). Do not overload the message if there is no need to do so as very bulky files can take a long time to send and receive.

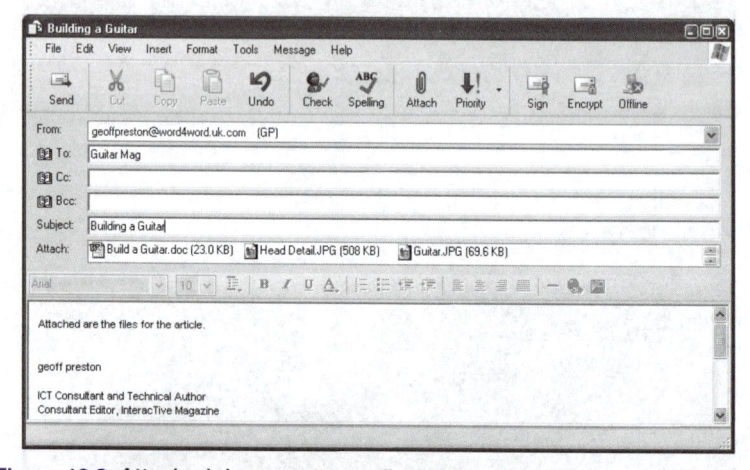

Figure 10.9 Attached documents are displayed in the Attach panel. In this case, three files (text, a picture and music) are attached.

Important

The right format If the person you are e-mailing cannot handle HTML format, send your message as an attachment, otherwise the enhancements may be lost. To get the most out of the enhancements, make sure the settings are configured correctly: **Tools, Options, Send, Reply to messages using the format in which they were sent**.

→ The Address Book

Entering the electronic address of a person you wish to contact can be carried out by the Outlook Express Address Book (Figure 10.10). This feature supplies you with the Internet addresses of your contacts.

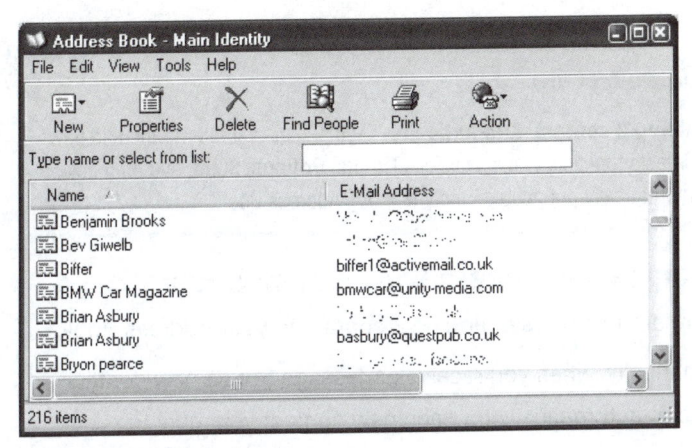

Figure 10.10 The Address Book.

Handling the Address Book

Click on **Address Book** in the Outlook Express toolbar. You can also do this via the message drafting window, by clicking the icon next to To.

Adding a new contact

You can add a contact manually by clicking **New, New Contact** on the toolbar. Enter the name and electronic address in the Name tab; you can also enter details of other contact information (Figure 10.11).

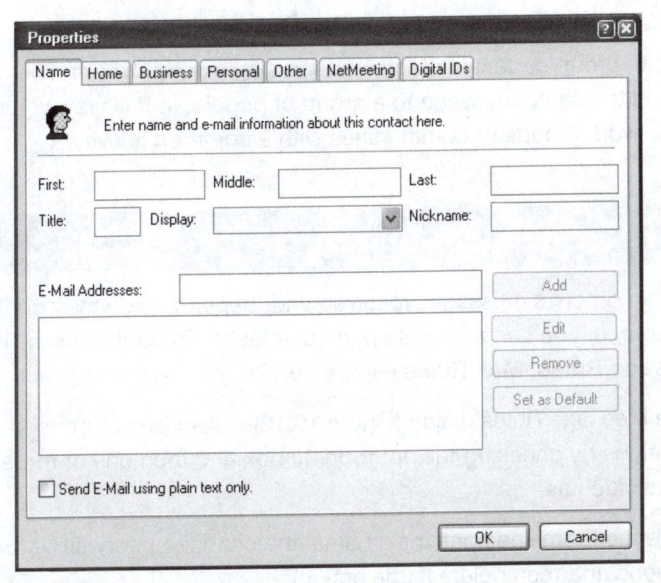

Figure 10.11 Entering details of a new contact.

Electronic mail 131

> **Timesaver tip**
>
> **Adding a contact automatically** You can also automate the add new contacts function as follows: select **Tools**, **Options**, **Send**, and then tick Automatically put people I reply to in my Address Book.

Filling in the Address Book automatically

There are two ways of adding a contact to your Address Book:

- manually, when you receive a message from a new contact
- semi-automatically for each new contact you reply to.

To add an address semi-automatically:

1. Position the mouse cursor on the message title.
2. Right-click, then click **Open** to activate it, or just double-click.
3. Point the mouse to the name of the sender.
4. Click the right button to display the context-sensitive menu.
5. Select Add to **Address Book**.
6. The Address Book window opens: make the necessary adjustments and confirm.

Setting up an electronic mailshot

You can group certain contacts under a single entry. This enables you to send the same message to a group of people. In this way, you can define work groups or communities with a common activity.

→ Filtering messages

You can process messages received and, depending on their contents and source, you can automate particular tasks. To do this, click **Tools**, **Message Rules**, **Mail Rules** (Figure 10.12).

In the Message Rules dialog (Figure 10.12), select one or more conditions by checking the appropriate box and then one or more actions such as:

Where the From line contains a name (the condition), forward it to someone and then delete it (the action).

> **Timesaver tip**
>
> **Handling your subscriptions effectively** If you subscribe to an online information service, you might find it useful to file the messages automatically in the same document folder. Use the '**from**' option for the sender as a condition and ask for the message to be moved to the folder. In this way, your Inbox will not be filled by subscriptions that you can read at your leisure from your customized folder.

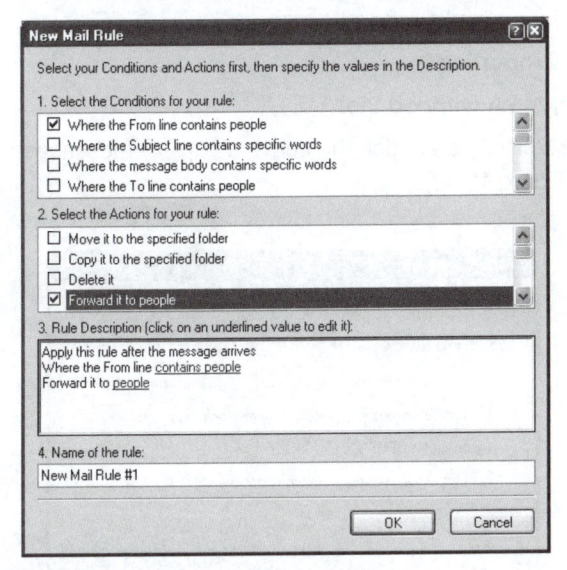

Figure 10.12 Setting up mail management rules.

When you have entered the actions and conditions, an outline appears in the bottom box. Some of the words will be underlined. These are links and clicking on them will open a dialog. For example, clicking on the word 'people' opens a window into which you enter an e-mail address.

→ Reading your mail from more than one computer

To manage your mail most efficiently from a portable and a desktop PC, you may retain it on the server when you look it up from the portable and copy it to the desktop PC for centralized reception. By default, the messages are copied from the server to the PC it is connected to. With these settings, the mail will be distributed among the various machines, depending on the connections set up, and you cannot get a central view of your messages. To block deletion of the message at the server end on one of the PCs, this is how you need to configure your software:

1 Activate the Tools menu.

2 Select **Accounts**.

3 Click the **Mail** tab.

4 Select your mail server.

5 Click **Properties**.

6 Select the **Advanced** tab.

7 In the Delivery area, tick the Leave a copy of messages on server box (Figure 10.13).

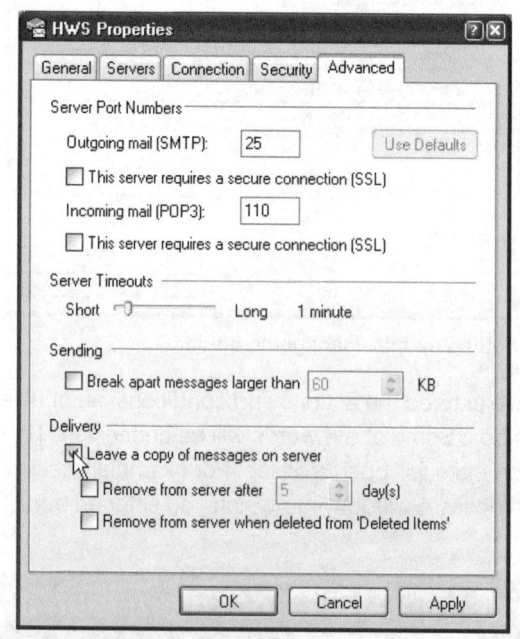

Figure 10.13 The mail remains stored in the server.

11 System tools

Windows XP is considered to be both more powerful and easier to use than its predecessors. With more high-performance settings and a faster shut down, the day-to-day operation of Windows has been greatly improved. As we saw in the installation procedure, these operations include technical monitoring of the PC to enhance performance and prevent problems.

→ Scheduled tasks

Tasks scheduled at installation time can be altered later. To do this, open the **Scheduled Tasks** folder from the Start menu by selecting **All Programs**, **Accessories**, **System Tools** (Figure 11.1).

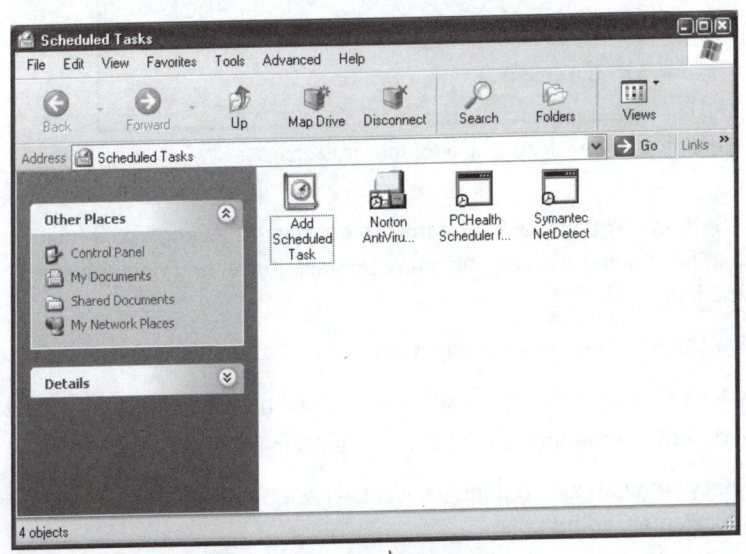

Figure 11.1 The scheduled system tasks folder.

To check a task, right-click on the relevant icon and click **Properties**. Three tabs are displayed:

- a task general description box
- the programming schedule (Figure 11.2)
- additional settings.

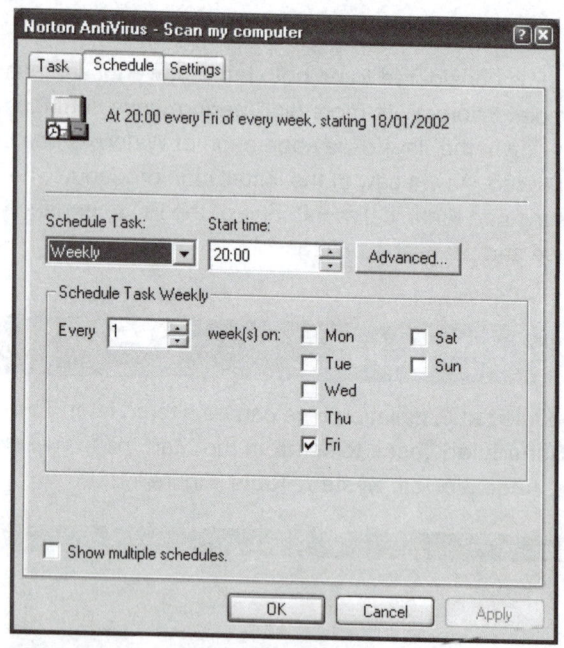

Figure 11.2 The task schedule for the virus scan.

In Settings, you can ask for a task to be deleted as soon as it has finished running. You can also halt the task at the end of a specified time limit.

You can also set the following rules:

- task start-up can only begin if the machine has been idle for x minutes
- do not run the task if the PC is currently in use.

Finally, you can also optimize the power supply resources (in the case of portables) so that:

- the task will not start if the PC is running on a battery
- the task shuts down as soon as the PC switches to battery mode.

In this way, you can modify or delete existing tasks. Back in the Scheduled Tasks dialog, click on **Add Scheduled Task**. This brings up the Scheduled Task Wizard (Figure 11.3).

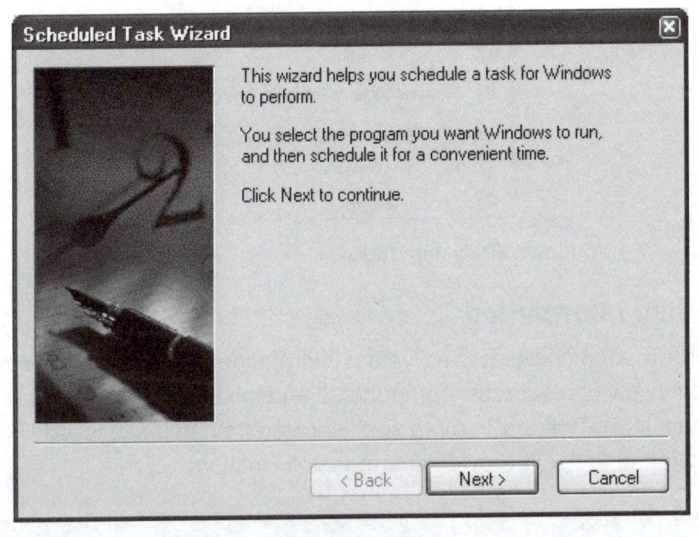

Figure 11.3 The Scheduled Task Wizard.

Once the wizard is up and running, click the programs you wish to run in Windows XP, e.g. select Outlook Express to schedule your mail reading routine. You indicate the frequency with which you want to run the program, every day for example.

Once you have configured the settings, select the Open advanced properties for this task when I click Finish box. You are then able to limit the task execution time. On completion of the settings, the task is added to the Scheduled Tasks folder. Windows XP now stays on continuous alert, ready to run the tasks you requested.

→ The system software

This can be accessed from the Start menu, through **All Programs**, **Accessories**, **System Tools** (Figure 11.4). Some of these tools will only be of interest to the more technically minded, but there are others that all users should know about.

- Activate Windows
- Character Map
- Clipboard Viewer
- Disk Cleanup
- Disk Defragmenter
- Files and Settings Transfer Wizard
- Scheduled Tasks
- System Information
- System Restore

Figure 11.4 Windows XP system tools.

System Information

Windows XP incorporates a System Information utility, which provides an overview of resources, components and the software environment (Figure 11.5). This tool is more sophisticated than that accessed from the Control Panel. It provides far more information.

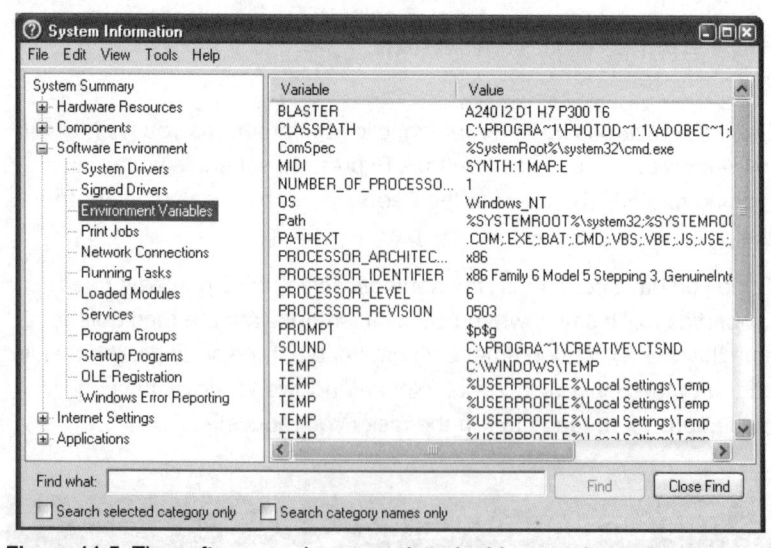

Figure 11.5 The software environment data, in this case the environment variables.

The pane on the left allows you to access the information headings, while the pane on the right displays the system data.

This utility contains a series of ActiveX checks, which collect the information requested and display it in the software.

The System Information tool is very powerful and enables you to carry out quick technical checks. If there is an operating problem with the PC, it can be used to detect any fault or a pilot version problem.

→ System Restore

With any luck you'll never need this, but it's good to know that it is there. Windows XP stores system restore points – backup copies of your important system files – at regular intervals. If these files become corrupted for any reason, whether it is user error, new software installation problems or hardware failure, System Restore will get your system running again.

To restore your system, go to the **System Tools** menu and select **System Restore**. At the first stage, select **Restore my computer ...** At the next panel, pick the most recent checkpoint when you know that the system was running properly.

Creating a restore point

A Windows XP computer is robust; modern software and hardware are normally reliable and thoroughly tested, but things do go wrong. Before you do anything which might upset the system, such as installing new hardware or software or making any other major changes, create a restore point. It takes only a few minutes and could save you endless hours of pain!

Start **System Restore** and select **Create a restore point**. Type in a description to help you identify it – the point will have the date and time added, so it is not too crucial to put that information in your description. Click **Next** to start the process.

Tidying up the hard disk

On start-up, this disk cleaning tool determines the spaces it can purge and therefore release on the hard disk. The Disk Cleanup window opens and indicates the volume (in megabytes) that can be released for each type of file (Figure 11.6). The evaluations are divided into file types:

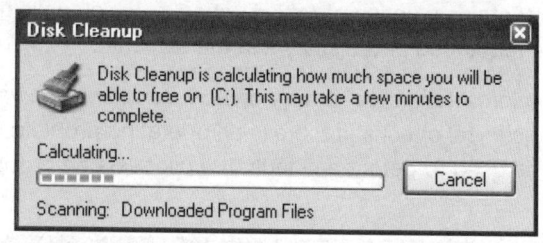

Figure 11.6 Determining the disk space that can be released.

- temporary Internet files
- files downloaded from the network
- files sent to the Recycle Bin
- temporary files
- Windows XP uninstall information files.

> **Important**
>
> **Uninstalling Windows XP** If you upgraded an older PC to Windows XP, do not delete the Windows XP uninstall files if you think you might want to revert to your old operating system at a later stage.

The More Options tab in the purging window is used either to delete unused Windows XP files, or to erase programs that are no longer used or to change the amount of disk space used by System Restore.

If you are removing a program, the software starts up the program uninstall window.

The FAT 32 converter

This is only of interest to people who have installed Windows XP over an earlier version of Windows.

This program is designed to convert the File Allocation Tables (FAT) to 32-bit format, thus bringing Windows XP into line with the Windows NT business family. This is a basic Windows 95 module, since it helps you manage hard disks of more than 2 Gb capacity more efficiently and improve the overall performance of your PC.

However, the decision to switch to the FAT 32 format is not an easy one and you are advised to read the online help on this subject before you start the procedure. You should be aware that some system utilities that work well with a FAT16 facility may no longer operate.

> **Important**
>
> **An irreversible conversion** If you choose to change to the 32-bit FAT mode, you will not be able to change back to 16-bit mode. Another consequence is that you will not be able to uninstall Windows XP from this point forward and revert to Windows 95. Progress is forward; you cannot go backwards.

Defragmenting the hard disk

By defragmenting your hard disk, you speed up subsequent processing. The aim is to store the data belonging to a particular file in a contiguous pattern. Any additions, modifications or deletions performed on all sorts of files (text, spreadsheet, database, etc.) generate pointers that provide a logical link between the data locations allocated to a given file. In effect, a particular file may have been created originally in an area of a given size and in the meantime that area may have been found to be too small to accommodate later additions. The additional data are stored in a vacant location away from the original file. So, defragmentation consists of reallocating adjacent spaces to various files.

The new defragmentation software keeps a record of the most frequently used files and keeps a close eye on the files generated by the program. It actually positions those files close to their respective programs, thereby improving performance and speed. Figure 11.7 shows the defragmenter in progress.

Checking the disk

This is one of the most frequently used system tools. It checks the files (file allocation tables, or FAT) and the surface of the hard disk. If your PC responds oddly, run this software straight away. There are two checking methods:

- a standard check of files and folders
- a more exacting check, which consists of analysing the disk surface (this can be quite a lengthy process, so you should run it when you do not need to use the PC).

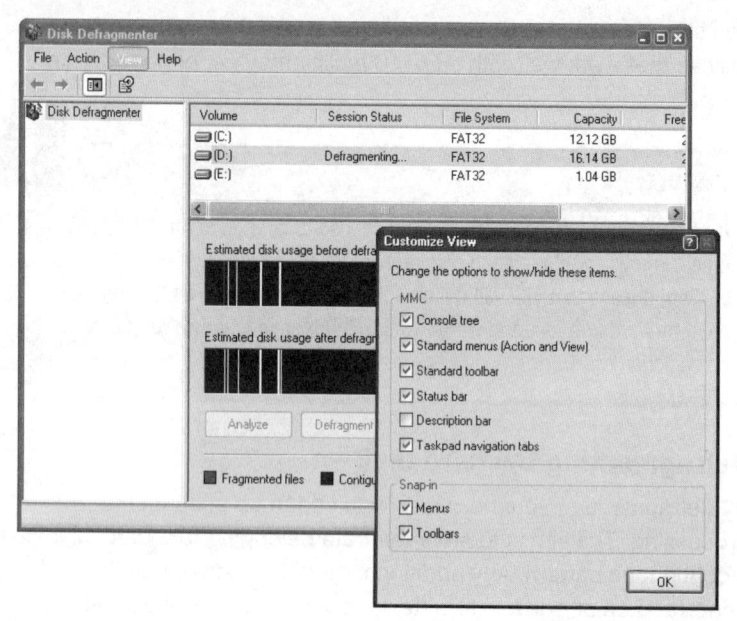

Figure 11.7 The defragmentation process, showing the customizing options dialog.

You can ask the software to correct errors automatically. If the error checking software will not start, it will probably be because the drive you are trying to check is in use. This is usually what happens when you try to check Drive C. An error message will be displayed announcing the fact and giving you the opportunity to have a test performed when you next switch on (Figure 11.8).

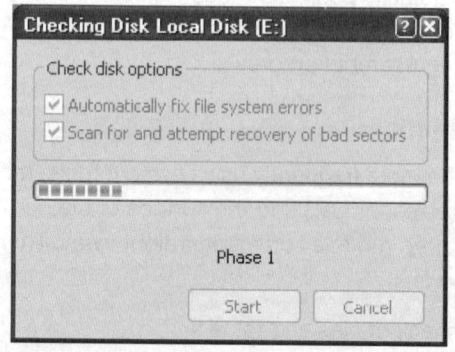

Figure 11.8 The first of a two-phase pass checking for errors.

→ Transferring settings

If you use more than one computer (e.g. one at home and another at the office, or networked computers), it makes sense to keep their settings similar. You can easily achieve this with the Files and Settings Transfer Wizard (Figure 11.9).

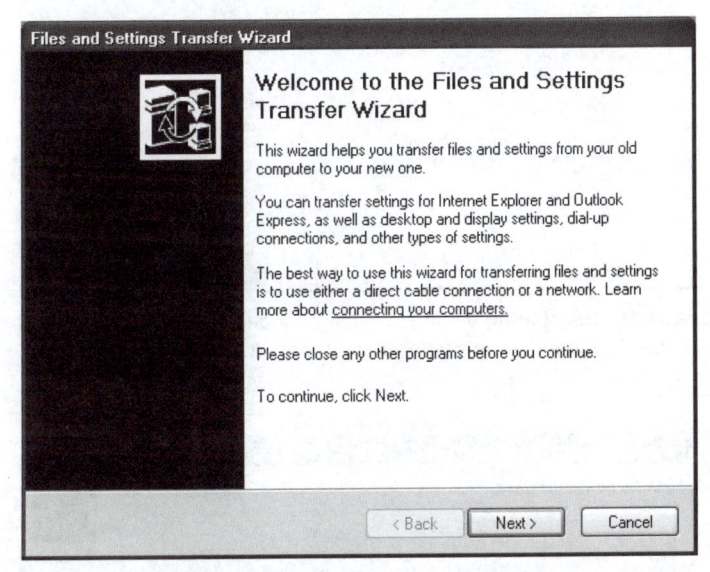

Figure 11.9 The wizard is found in Accessories, System Tools.

On the computer on which you are working, decide whether you want to transfer settings to another computer, or import settings from another computer. If you are transferring settings from another networked computer, it can be running virtually any version of Microsoft Windows, except 3.11.

After a short while, you must choose the method of transfer to the other computer. It could be floppy disk, but a larger-capacity disk like a writeable CD-ROM would be preferable. If the two computers are networked, you can send the files that way.

You then choose to transfer either settings, or files, or both files and settings (Figure 11.10).

When the drive containing the settings file(s) has been inserted into the off-site computer, you can load them and the selected applications will inherit the same settings as the other computer (Figure 11.11).

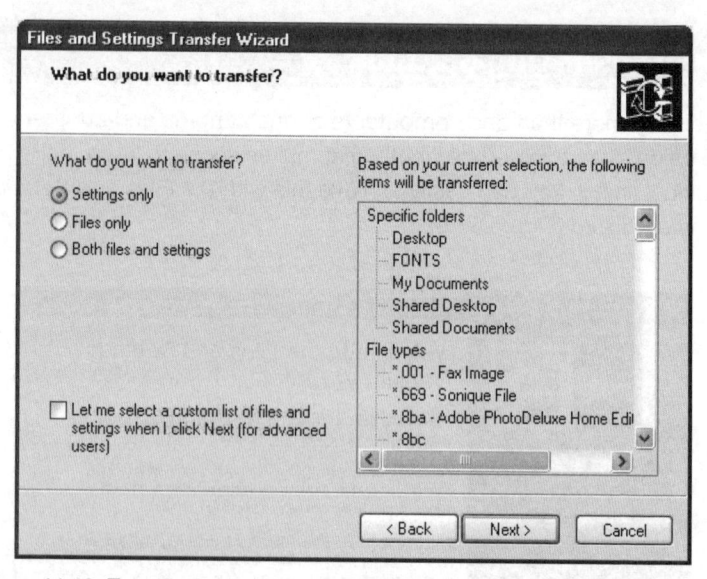

Figure 11.10 Transferring settings to a high-capacity removable drive which can be taken to another computer at a different location.

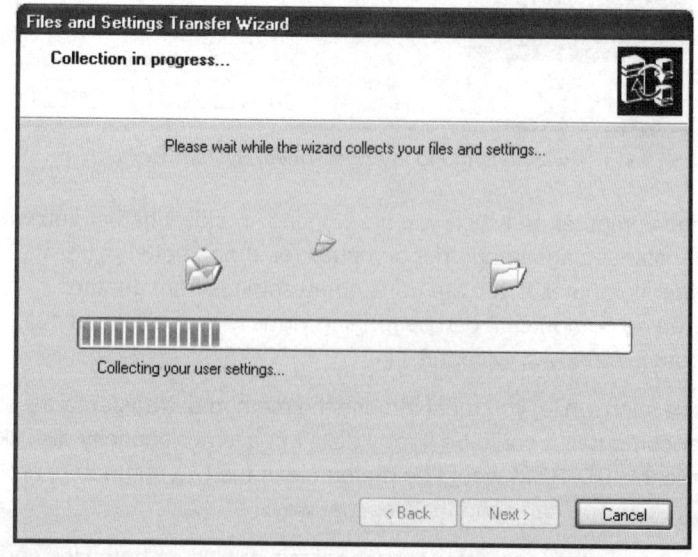

Figure 11.11 Moving the settings from one computer to another.

12 Windows XP and multimedia applications

Compression is the multimedia spearhead on a PC. Without compression, just wave goodbye to the whole notion. For example, by compressing music files, you can quarter file sizes while keeping a sound quality close to that of an audio CD. The compression methods employed do not result in any appreciable loss of quality. Only experienced music-lovers will detect the difference between the two recordings.

> **Information**
>
> **Audio compression** Sound, like video, gobbles up disk space. For example, one second of CD-quality music requires about 170 kilobytes of storage space. To prevent your hard disk becoming full, you need to use sound compression algorithms.

Some audio compression tools are designed to process voice. This applies, in particular, to TrueSpeech, a process that allows you to compress voice signals and record them on the hard disk in real time. The TrueSpeech compression ratio is significant, because the frequency range used to reproduce faithfully the human voice is very narrow.

Whether for music or voice, compression opens up new horizons. Space-saving on the hard disk is not the only objective – far from it, because multimedia transmissions and networks have to be taken into account.

Windows XP also incorporates all the resources needed to handle video in digital format (AVI – audiovideo interleave). Different compression methods (codecs) are available, including MPEG-oriented methods. This latter technology, which consumes vast decompression resources, normally requires the installation of a dedicated compression board.

In Windows XP, everything has been done to improve multimedia facilities and to assist their use. The AutoPlay mode (which appeared originally in Windows 95) is a typical example.

→ AutoPlay mode for CD-ROMs

When you insert an audio compact disk in your hi-fi, the system automatically goes to the first track and plays the piece. So, why do we need to install a CD-ROM? And when it has been used once, why do we have to go back to the control to run it again?

With AutoPlay mode, when you insert a CD-ROM in your drive, Windows XP checks whether an Autorun.inf file exists; if so, the file is executed. Otherwise, Windows XP carries out an automated installation procedure, creates the start-up file and runs it, without the need for you to do anything. Simply inserting the disk means that you want to 'play' it. So, Windows XP takes over all the tasks which, until now, you had to carry out yourself.

Information

The MIDI standard for music The MIDI standard is important for music files. Music scores enable us to describe a Beethoven sonata in just a few pages. But to play it, you need a quality piano and a talented interpreter. MIDI files resemble scores: they are control files that enable us to 'describe' music concisely.

→ Multimedia utilities

Windows XP is supplied with a number of multimedia utilities, which you can call up from Start, All Programs, Accessories, Entertainment.

→ Media Player

Media Player is the standard Windows XP multipurpose audio/video player. It can handle sound files in MIDI and in the native Windows format, WAVE – as well as audio CDs and the popular MP3. It also plays video in the standard AVI format, Media Audio/Video (WMA and ASF) and many ActiveMovie formats.

> **Information**
>
> **MP3** MP3 is a very popular music format which compresses CD-quality music by removing frequencies the human ear cannot hear. MP3 files can be played using Windows Media Player and also on an ever-increasing number of portable devices, including some mobile phones.

CD Audio

If Media Player is not running, it will start up and play an audio CD when you insert it into the drive. If it is already running, then to play a CD, click the CD Audio button, insert the CD and wait for a moment for Media Player to read the track information.

The CD will play the tracks in the playlist sequence – initially this will be the standard order. To change the order of tracks, click on one to select it, then drag up or down. To skip over tracks, select them, then right-click and choose Disable from the shortcut menu (Figure 12.1).

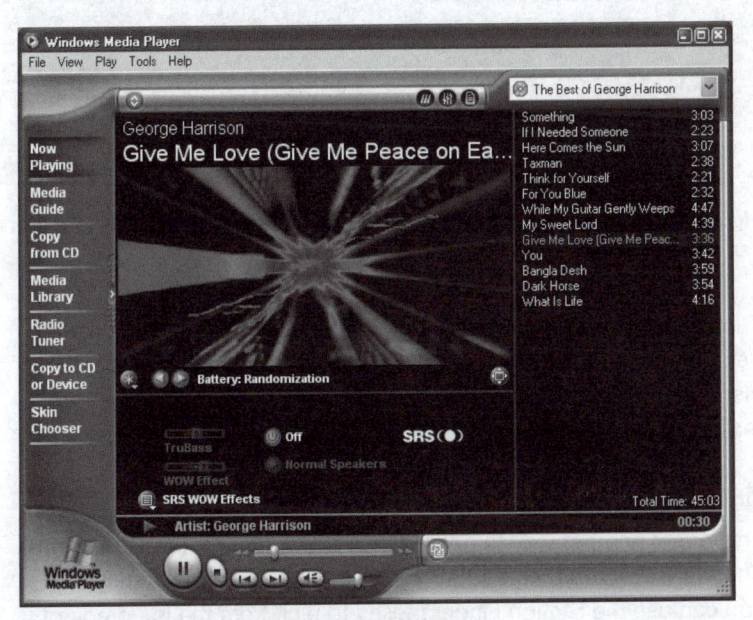

Figure 12.1 Media Player playing an audio CD.

Windows XP and multimedia applications   **147**

Any choices or other information that you enter here are recorded by Windows XP in a file (on the hard disk) and will be reused next time the same CD is loaded.

Once the playlist is set up and the CD is playing, you can switch into compact mode. This doesn't just occupy less screen space, it also has some great 'skins' (window designs – Figure 12.2). Select a skin from the View, Taskbar, Skin Chooser display.

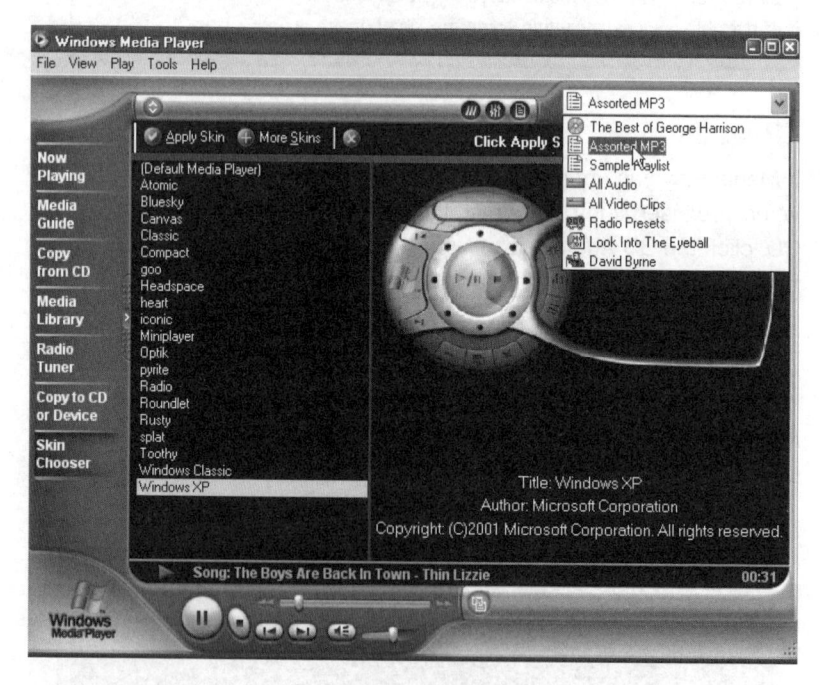

Figure 12.2 There are a dozen Media Player skins to choose from, and you can find more at Microsoft's Web site.

When a CD is playing, a 'visualization' is shown. If you don't like the default there are plenty of alternatives. Open the View menu, point to Visualization, select a set then pick from there. The names are not terribly helpful – you'll have to watch them to make a proper choice.

Radio

This offers another way to get radio over the Internet (see Chapter 9). There are a dozen pre-set stations, catering to a range of tastes, or you can use the Station Finder facility to pick from the hundreds of stations that are now broadcasting. You will find, when choosing a station, that Internet Explorer will normally open to show you the station's Web site. This can be closed down, if not wanted, to save screen space and speed up download of the broadcast.

Obviously, if you are paying for your phone time when you are online, this is not an efficient way to listen to the radio!

Video

Newer, faster hardware and more efficient software has significantly improved the quality of videos on PC, but they are still small and jerky – or run them in full-screen mode and they are large and blocky and jerky!

The main sources of videos are multimedia packages, where Media Player can be called up automatically to play the clips, demos and samples on CDs, and – most of all – the Internet.

There are three main ways in which you will get video from the Internet:

- Clips for downloading – the new high-compression formats have brought a better balance between download time and playing time. 1 Mb of video gives you around 90 seconds of playing time, and will take up to 10 minutes to download – and you must have the whole file on your disk before you can start to play it.
- Streaming video in TV and webcam broadcasts and, increasingly, in movie and pop video clips. Here the videos are played as they download. The images are jerkier, but at least you don't have to wait to see whether they are worth watching at all.
- Home movies e-mailed to you by relatives, who also have Windows XP and have been playing with its Movie Maker (see page 149).

Portable device

CD audio tracks and files, from the Internet or elsewhere, in MP3, WAV, WMA or ASF formats can be copied through Media Player on to your MP3 player or other portable device.

The Sound Recorder

The Windows XP Sound Recorder reproduces the conventional interface of a real sound recorder, with the addition of a screen to display a graphic curve of the sound emitted (Figure 12.3).

Figure 12.3 The Windows XP Sound Recorder.

To record music or speech, you should first connect an audio source or a microphone to the sound board line input. Adjust the sound quality settings as required. To do this, click on Edit, Audio Properties. You can then set the recording conditions.

Then follow these steps:

1 From the File menu, click New to open a blank file.
2 Then click the record button (the red circle).
3 Finally, click on the black square to stop recording.

You can then check the recording by playing it back (the single, black triangle).

In the File menu, click Save As to save the sound file on the PC hard disk.

From the Effects menu, you can increase or decrease the volume, adjust the echo, or even invert sounds. These few features allow you to create all sorts of special sound effects.

You can only add an echo and invert the sound signal on an uncompressed file. The same applies to adjusting the volume level. You can modify the initial quality of a sound with the converter incorporated in the sound recorder. To do this, click File, Properties.

The sound recorder is a genuine mixing panel that also enables you to record a sound in a sound file. To do so, open a sound file and go to the position you want using the cursor and pressing Pause on play. Then start your recording. In this way, you can insert a sound file in another sound file or mix the sounds.

Overall volume adjustment

The volume control can be called up directly or from a multimedia accessory. It can also be accessed via the icon at the right-hand side of the Taskbar. It allows you to adjust the volume for all the audio devices in your PC (Figure 12.4). To alter the volume, slide the vertical bar. The horizontal cursor is used to set the balance between the loudspeakers.

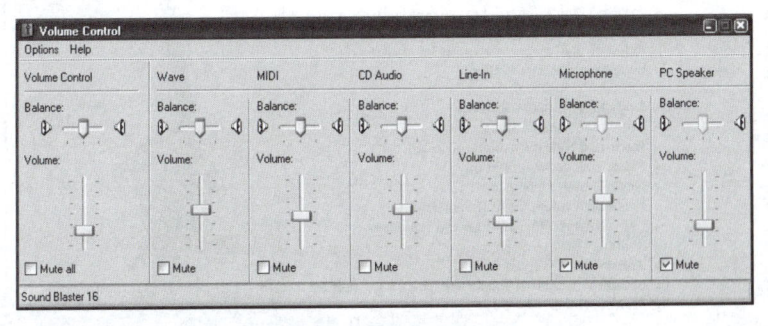

Figure 12.4 Adjusting the volume of audio devices.

The volume and balance controls affect WAV files, MIDI files, the audio CD, the line input and even your microphone or loudspeakers. In Options, Properties you can tick the devices to be displayed and call up the volume control for playback, recording or voice commands.

→ Plug-ins and players

With the help of software search and compression techniques, the multimedia phenomenon has surfaced on the Web to the point where we now talk of Web channels, rather than Web sites. Of course, marketing accounts for much of this, but we should not ignore the facts: computer animation, audio and video have had a profound effect on the Web.

Even with our good old telephone line on the Public Switched Telephone Network (PSTN), we can benefit from the wealth of multimedia facilities offered by the Web. To do this, you need two sorts of tools:

- plug-ins
- players.

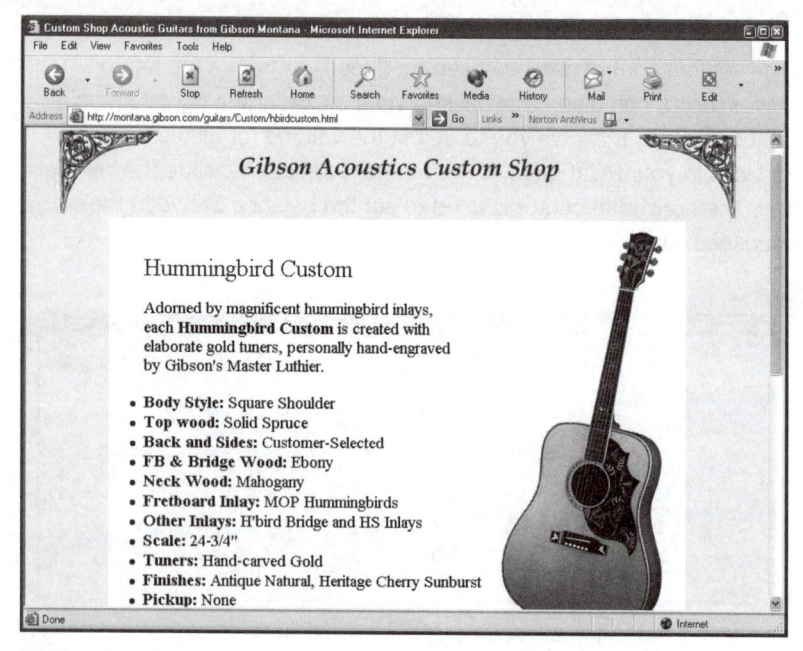

Figure 12.5 This guitar site offers visitors the chance to listen to the instruments.

These names conceal very simple concepts. A plug-in is a small program that is placed in the browser in order to run certain features, such as executing a computer animation. This is what is done by Real Audio and Real Video from Progressive Networks (Figure 12.5).

A player is a stand-alone software package responsible for meeting requirements that the browser cannot offer as standard, such as playing audio or video files available on the Web. Media Player can cope with many formats, but you may find it worthwhile to get a copy of Quicktime from Apple (www.apple.com) as many video clips are in Quicktime format.

Of course, other technologies are available and, to make the most of them, you should from time to time load the plug-ins that have been incorporated in the Internet Explorer 6.0 browser.

→ Audio and video

Audio and video are new features on the Web. The bandwidth of the telephone network currently does not allow you to display video in real time in optimum conditions, with the result that playing video is slow and image quality is poor. You have to settle for smaller documents with image refresh once a second at best.

> **Important**
>
> **Listening to the radio on the Web** For this you need a quality modem connection: at least 28.8 Kbps and a PC with a good configuration. Needless to say, microwave radio stations have seized upon this technology. Today, hundreds of radio stations throughout the world offer 'live' listening from their transmitters. While direct hi-fi broadcasting has not yet arrived, it is still possible to download audio programmes using high fidelity technology.

Consequently, on the Web, audio is overtaking video because it requires fewer resources. We should distinguish between two sorts of audio-video application:

- **Offline**. The files are downloaded to the PC and then played locally.
- **Real time, or 'live'**. The sources are played back directly from the Web, without storing them in the PC.

While real-time video at present is something of a misnomer, real-time audio – radio, in effect – works perfectly well.

> **Information**
>
> **Hi-fi on your PC** The tools required to play a CD-ROM (or audio CD), or video clip, or adjust the volume control, can be called up in the Entertainment menu in the Accessories folder (through Start and Programs). This is also where you access the DVD player software.

→ Movie Maker

This software is new with Windows XP. You can use Movie Maker to edit digital video, taking images in directly from your camera (Figure 12.6). The software can sense the change of scenes and will split the video into clips for you. The clips can then be split further or trimmed and set into a new sequence. You can merge in other video clips, or

Figure 12.6 Movie Maker being used to edit a file.

add still pictures, for titles and credits, or a voice-over or background music. Movie Maker has all the essential editing suite facilities to allow you to produce good movies, if you have the time and the skill.

The Movie Maker format takes around 10 Kb for each second of playing time. This means that while video files are not small, they are very much more compact than the ones produced by older formats. Sharing videos with distant friends and relatives via the Internet is now quite feasible. There are two ways to do it:

- Send the movie by e-mail. Files are increased in size by 50% when attached to a message (because of the way that data are transferred through the mail system), but you can normally download e-mail at 3 Kb or more per second.
- Upload the file to your home page, and send the URL to people. This allows people the choice of whether they want to spend time getting your video, but download times from the Web are typically less than 2 Kb per second through dial-up lines. You will need at least a basic grasp of making Web pages to be able to do this.

What it boils down to is that it is going to take your distant friends and relatives around one minute to download 100 Kb of video, which will play for 10 seconds.

→ Playing DVDs

Windows XP comes ready to cater for the new generation of very high capacity disks, in this case the DVD (digital versatile disk), which allows you to show films and multimedia programmes on your PC.

DVD drives use USB or IEEE 1394 type connections. Once the drive has been fitted in your PC, you should configure the settings or make Windows XP recognize it automatically (use the Add Hardware icon in the Control Panel).

Finally, you need to install the DVD player supplied with Windows XP. To do this, go to the Control Panel again, click Add/Remove Programs, then select the Windows set-up tab. In the Multimedia window, check the DVD Player box and start the installation process from the Windows XP CD-ROM.